THE
PRACTICE
OF
WISDOM

THE
PRACTICE
OF
WISDOM

A Topical Guide to Proverbs

RONALD M. SAILLER
DAVID WYRTZEN

MOODY PRESS

CHICAGO

ISBN: 0-8024-6896-9

1 3 5 7 9 10 8 6 4 2

Printed in the United States of America

This book is dedicated in loving memory to Gary C. Sabin,
who went to be with the Lord on July 9, 1990.
Gary attended Calvary Bible College at the same time
Ron did and his love for the Lord was
evident to all those who knew him.
"The memory of the righteous will be a blessing"
(Proverbs 10:7a)

CONTENTS

ACKNOWLEDGMENTS

Special thanks goes to a number of people whose contributions made this book possible. These include Alison Ogran for typing the first and second draft and Ron's sister Diane Sailler for her many hours word processing the final revision of the book.

To Warren E. Bathke, Robert L. Domokas, Francis M. Hanna, Phil Henderson, Ray Hildebrand, Leslie Madison, Jan Metheny, Kenneth L. Powell, Larry Spry, Joe Zanatta, Marty Zide, and the elders at Southwest Bible Church, Prairie Village, Kansas—thanks to all for the advice, encouragement, and general interest.

INTRODUCTION

Does the Bible prepare us only for a heavenly life divorced from the sweat, tears, and laughter of earthly living? What does God have to say about problems like alcoholism, poverty, unjust courts, and insensitive corporate bosses? What about taking care of pets, or balancing our check books? Does God care about these mundane necessities? Proverbs is God's answer, and *The Practice of Wisdom* is a tool to lead us to biblical answers to these kinds of realistic questions.

We have presented forty-two major themes of Proverbs and organized the applicable verses under appropriate sub-headings. The *New International Version* of the Bible has been used for all Scripture quotations. Here is easy access to God's eternal principles for practical living. Suppose you face the frustration of dealing with a lazy relative who continually mooches but refuses to find a job. Simply check out the theme "Laziness." There you will find, printed out and organized, a comprehensive list of all the verses in Proverbs dealing with that subject. Or perhaps you received a gracious gift from a faithful friend and you would like to respond with an appropriate verse on your thank you note. Simply look up "Friendships" and read through the verses until you find the response that is right for your friend. Have you ever discussed the proper way to discipline children, but could not recall where the verses in Proverbs dealing with "Discipline" or "Family Relationships" could be found? Do you know where God discusses what teenagers need to know about sexual love? This study guide places these verses before you. Read, meditate, memorize—the sections on the family and morality alone could preserve your home. The sections on "Wisdom" and "Foolishness" could preserve your life.

As each of the forty-two themes begins a brief summary presents the essential principles derived from the selected verses that follow. The reference numbers to the right of each verse are keyed to *The NIV Exhaustive Concordance* (Grand Rapids: Zondervan, 1990). These numbers indicate which Hebrew word(s) is being translated by the indexed words. From this concordance certain abbreviations and symbols used with the reference numbers have been adopted. They are explained as follows:

NIH ("not in Hebrew") indicates the indexed word was supplied for clarity in translation.

AIT ("assists in translation") indicates the indexed word (shown in italics) assists the word shown in roman bold type.

Plus (+) indicates the indexed English word translates more than one word in the Hebrew.

Slash (/) separates reference numbers for successive indexed words in a single verse or passage.

Raised "s" (ˢ) indicates the indexed word is a substitutionary translation for stylistic reasons.

At the end of the book the Index cross-references each principle found under all the individual themes. Thus you can trace the subject further throughout Proverbs.

May the God of all wisdom richly bless you and pour out His wisdom to you as you search for it as for hidden treasures (Prov. 2:4).

RONALD M. SAILLER
DAVID B. WYRTZEN

ALCOHOL

Alcohol—the most abused substance in our contemporary culture—causes more deaths than AIDS, heroin, cocaine, marijuana, and crack combined. When poured on a wound this good gift from the Creator can destroy germs. When too much is poured into the body, it poisons a life. God's skillful moral instruction hammers home a warning statement—alcohol is addictive, deceitful, unjust, lazy, unfeeling, cruel, and violent.

		REFERENCE NUMBERS
ALCOHOL AND ADDICTION		
Wake Up		
23:35	"They hit me," you will say, "but I'm not hurt! They beat me, but I don't feel it! When will I **wake up** so I can find another drink?"	7810
Wine		
23:30	Those who linger over **wine**, who go to sample bowls of mixed **wine**.	3516/4932
ALCOHOL AND DECEIT		
Beer		
20:1	wine is a mocker and **beer** a brawler; whoever is led astray by them is not wise.	8911
Drink		
23:7	for he is the kind of man who is always thinking about the cost. "Eat and **drink**," he says to you, but his heart is not with you.	9272
ALCOHOL AND AUTHORITIES		
Drink		
31:4	"It is not for kings, O Lemuel—not for kings to **drink** wine, not for rulers to crave beer"	9272
31:5	lest they **drink** and forget what the law decrees, and deprive all the oppressed of their rights.	9272
ALCOHOL AND THE POOR		
Drink		
23:20	Do not join those who **drink** too much wine or gorge themselves on meat,	6010
31:7	let them **drink** and forget their poverty and remember their misery no more.	9272
Drunkard		
23:21	for **drunkards** and gluttons become poor, and drowsiness clothes them in rags.	6010
Wine		
20:1	**Wine** is a mocker and beer a brawler; whoever is led astray by them is not wise.	3516
21:17	He who loves pleasure will become poor; whoever loves **wine** and oil will never be rich.	3516
ALCOHOL AND INSENSITIVITY		
Drunkard		
26:9	Like a thornbush in a **drunkard's** hand is a proverb in the mouth of a fool.	8893

Wake Up
23:35   "They hit me," you will say, "but I'm not hurt! They beat me,   7810
        but I don't feel it! When will I **wake up** so I can find another
        drink?"

ALCOHOL AND SOBRIETY

Wine
23:31   Do not gaze at **wine** when it is red, when it sparkles in the cup,   3516
        when it goes down smoothly!

ALCOHOL AND VIOLENCE

Bloodshot
23:29   Who has woe? Who has sorrow? Who has strife? Who has   2680
        complaints? Who has needless bruises? Who has **bloodshot**
        eyes?

Violence
4:17   They eat the bread of wickedness and drink the wine of **vio-**   2805
        lence.

10:6   Blessings crown the head of the righteous, but **violence** over-   2805
        whelms the mouth of the wicked.

Wake Up
23:35   "They hit me," you will say, "but I'm not hurt! They beat me,   7810
        but I don't feel it! When will I **wake up** so I can find another
        drink?"

ANIMALS AND INSECTS

In the Creator's biology class, animals and insects are not viewed as the products of chance and evolutionary development—specimens only to be dissected and classified. Instead, their habits are to be carefully observed, for here the designer of life provides object lessons that can teach us how to live wisely. Proverbs uses animals to illustrate everything from sex ethics to economics. Enroll in this course and allow the pre-eminent naturalist in the universe to expose not only the world of animals but also the realities of human life and culture.

REFERENCE
NUMBERS

ANIMALS AND ALCOHOL

Snake/Viper
23:32   In the end it bites like a **snake** and poisons like a **viper**.   5729/7626

ANIMALS AND DISCIPLINE

Horse/Donkey
26:3   A whip for the **horse**, a halter for the **donkey**, and a rod for the   6061/2789
backs of fools!

ANIMALS AND THE FOOL

Bear
17:12   Better to meet a **bear** robbed of her cubs than a fool in his folly.   1800
Dog
26:11   As a **dog** returns to its vomit, so a fool repeats his folly.   3978
26:17   Like one who seizes a **dog** by the ears is a passer-by who med-   3978
dles in a quarrel not his own.

ANIMALS AND AUTHORITIES

Lion
19:12   A king's rage is like the roar of a **lion**, but his favor is like dew   4097
on the grass.
20:2   A king's wrath is like the roar of a **lion**; he who angers him for-   4097
feits his life.
Lion/Bear
28:15   Like a roaring **lion** or a charging **bear** is a wicked man ruling   787/1800
over a helpless people.
Lizard
30:28   a **lizard** can be caught with the hand, yet it is found in kings'   8532
palaces.
Locust
30:27   **locusts** have no king, yet they advance together in ranks;   746

ANIMALS AND WISDOM

Coney
30:26   **coneys** are creatures of little power, yet they make their home   9176
in the crags;
Eagle/Snake
30:19   the way of an **eagle** in the sky, the way of a **snake** on a rock,   5979/5729
the way of a ship on the high seas, and the way of a man with a
maiden.

ANIMALS AND THE RIGHTEOUS

Animal

12:10   A righteous man cares for the needs of his **animal**, but the kin-   989
dest acts of the wicked are cruel.

Lion

28:1   The wicked man flees though no one pursues, but the righteous   4097
are as bold as a **lion**.

ANIMALS AND STRENGTH

Horse

21:31   The **horse** is made ready for the day of battle, but victory rests   6061

Lion/Beast with the LORD.

30:30   a **lion**, mighty among **beasts**, who retreats before nothing;   4330/989

ANIMALS AND THE FAMILY

Doe/Deer

5:19   A loving **doe**, a graceful **deer**—may her breasts satisfy you al-   387/3607
ways, may you ever be captivated by her love.

Raven/Vulture

30:17   "The eye that mocks a father, that scorns obedience to a moth-   6854/
er, will be pecked out by the **ravens** of the valley, will be eaten   1201 + 5979
by the **vultures**."

ANIMALS AND PROVISIONS

Lamb/Goat

27:26   the **lambs** will provide you with clothing, and the **goats** with   3897/6966
the price of a field.

ANIMALS AND LAZINESS

Lion

22:13   The sluggard says, "There is a **lion** outside!" or, "I will be   787
murdered in the streets!"

26:13   The sluggard says, "There is a **lion** in the road, a fierce **lion**   8828/787
roaming the streets!"

ANIMALS AND IMMORALITY

Ox/Deer/Bird

7:22-23   All at once he followed her like an **ox** going to the slaughter,   8802/385/
like a **deer** stepping into a noose [23] till an arrow pierces his   7606
liver, like a **bird** darting into a snare, little knowing it will cost
him his life.

ANIMALS AND HATRED

Calf

15:17   Better a meal of vegetables where there is love than a fattened   8802
calf with hatred.

Sparrow/Swallow

26:2   Like a fluttering **sparrow** or a darting **swallow**, an undeserved   7606/2000
curse does not come to rest.

INSECTS AND DILIGENCE

Ant

| 6:6-8 | Go to the **ant**, you sluggard; consider its ways and be wise! [7] It has no commander, no overseer or ruler, [8] yet it stores its provisions in summer and gathers its food at harvest. | 5805 |
| 30:25 | **Ants** are creatures of little strength, yet they store up their food in the summer; | 5805 |

APPEARANCE

In a society built on appearances we need to hear that clothes, cosmetics, and physical attractiveness do not make the man or the woman. A reverent relationship with God is worth far more than being a "perfect 10." Aware of the need for balance, our wisdom teacher does not denigrate physical appearance. God x-rays the heart, but we can discern the inside only by carefully observing the outward signs. Like a skillful detective, the keen observer of faces can discover cheerfulness and love, and sometimes anger and hatred in just the look of the eye or a change in facial expression. To discern the countenance of another might save you your job, or even your life.

REFERENCE
NUMBERS

APPEARANCE AND IMMORALITY

Beauty
6:25   Do not lust in your heart after her **beauty** or let her captivate   3642
you with her eyes,

APPEARANCE AND OLD AGE

Splendor
20:29   The glory of young men is their strength, gray hair the **splen-**   2077
dor of the old.

APPEARANCE AND THE FEAR OF THE LORD

Beauty
31:30   Charm is deceptive, and **beauty** is fleeting; but a woman who   3642
fears the Lord is to be praised.

APPEARANCE AND FACIAL EXPRESSION

Cheerful
15:13   A happy heart makes the face **cheerful**, but heartache crushes   3512
the spirit.

Sly
25:23   As a north wind brings rain, so a **sly** tongue brings angry looks.   6260

APPEARANCE AND AUTHORITIES

Face
16:15   When a king's **face** brightens, it means life; his favor is like a   7156
rain cloud in spring.

AUTHORITIES

An authority is a leader entrusted with responsibility for others. From court rooms to board rooms governmental and business leaders should exhibit justice, honesty, diligence, compassion, and courtesy in executing their divinely ordained governing functions. The ancient monarchial form of government, assumed in Proverbs, differs greatly from a modern democracy, but Solomon's stress on generic ethics for leaders gives timely insight into normative principles that enable any form of government, or leadership, to meet the needs of its people. God's Word remains the source of all legitimate authority, and respect for authority derives from respect for the Bible.

		REFERENCE
AUTHORITIES AND THE POOR		NUMBERS

Judge

29:14	If a king **judges** the poor with fairness, his throne will always be secure.	9149
31:9	"Speak up and **judge** fairly; defend the rights of the poor and needy."	9149

Ruler

22:7	The rich **rule** over the poor, and the borrower is servant to the lender.	5440
28:15	Like a roaring lion or a charging bear is a wicked man **ruling** over a helpless people.	5440
28:16	A tyrannical **ruler** lacks judgment, but he who hates ill-gotten gain will enjoy a long life.	5592

AUTHORITIES AND HONOR

King

14:28	A large population is a **king's** glory, but without subjects a prince is ruined.	4889
16:13	**Kings** take pleasure in honest lips; they value a man who speaks the truth.	4889
25:6	Do not exalt yourself in the **king's** presence, and do not claim a place among great men;	4889
31:3	do not spend your strength on women, your vigor on those who ruin **kings**.	4889

Master

27:18	He who tends a fig tree will eat its fruit, and he who looks after his **master** will be honored.	123

Nobleman

25:7	it is better for him to say to you, "Come up here," than for him to humiliate you before a **nobleman**.	5618

Official

17:26	It is not good to punish an innocent man, or to flog **officials** for their integrity.	5618

Ruler

23:1	When you sit to dine with a **ruler**, note well what is before you,	5440

AUTHORITIES AND JUDGMENT

King

14:35	A **king** delights in a wise servant, but a shameful servant incurs his wrath.	4889

		REFERENCE NUMBERS
16:10	The lips of a **king** speak as an oracle, and his mouth should not betray justice.	4889
16:14	A **king's** wrath is a messenger of death, but a wise man will appease it.	4889
16:15	When a **king's** face brightens, it means life; his favor is like a rain cloud in spring.	8356
19:12	A **king's** rage is like the roar of a lion, but his favor is like dew on the grass.	4889
20:2	A **king's** wrath is like the roar of a lion; he who angers him forfeits his life.	4889
20:8	When a **king** sits on his throne to judge, he winnows out all evil with his eyes.	4889
20:26	A wise **king** winnows out the wicked; he drives the threshing wheel over them.	4889
25:2	It is the glory of God to conceal a matter; to search out a matter is the glory of **kings**.	4889
25:5	remove the wicked from the **king's** presence, and his throne will be established through righteousness.	4889
29:4	By justice a **king** gives a country stability, but one who is greedy for bribes tears it down.	4889

Master

30:10	"Do not slander a servant to his **master**, or he will curse you, and you will pay for it."	123

Ruler

25:15	Through patience a **ruler** can be persuaded, and a gentle tongue can break a bone.	7903

AUTHORITIES AND OBEDIENCE

King

14:35	A **king** delights in a wise servant, but a shameful servant incurs his wrath.	4889
16:14	A **king's** wrath is a messenger of death, but a wise man will appease it.	4889
19:12	A **king's** rage is like the roar of a lion, but his favor is like dew on the grass.	4889
24:21	Fear the LORD and the **king**, my son, and do not join with the rebellious,	4889

Master

25:13	Like the coolness of snow at harvest time is a trustworthy messenger to those who send him; he refreshes the spirit of his **masters**.	123

Ruler

19:6	Many curry favor with a **ruler**, and everyone is the friend of a man who gives gifts.	5618
29:26	Many seek an audience with a **ruler**, but it is from the LORD that man gets justice.	5440

AUTHORITIES AND HONESTY

King

16:12	**Kings** detest wrongdoing, for a throne is established through righteousness.	4889

16:13	**Kings** take pleasure in honest lips; they value a man who speaks the truth.	4889
20:28	Love and faithfulness keep a **king** safe; through love his throne is made secure.	4889
22:11	He who loves a pure heart and whose speech is gracious will have the **king** for his friend.	4889

Ruler

17:7	Arrogant lips are unsuited to a fool—how much worse lying lips to a **ruler**!	5618
28:2	When a country is rebellious, it has many **rulers**, but a man of understanding and knowledge maintains order.	8569
29:12	If a **ruler** listens to lies, all his officials become wicked.	5440

AUTHORITIES AND SOBRIETY

King

31:4	"It is not for **kings**, O Lemuel—not for **kings** to drink wine, not for rulers to crave beer"	4889

AUTHORITIES AND WORK

Ruler

12:24	Diligent hands will **rule**, but laziness ends in slave labor.	5440
17:2	A wise servant will **rule** over a disgraceful son, and will share the inheritance as one of the brothers.	5440

King

22:29	Do you see a man skilled in his work? He will serve before **kings**; he will not serve before obscure men.	4889

BLESSINGS

Unlike human speech, God's words convey power. In Proverbs He pronounces His powerful word of favor over the lives of those who follow His instructions for skillful living. In the home, government, and business, success comes to those who trust God. The New Testament reaffirms this blessing upon those who believe: "anyone who comes to him must believe that he exists and that he rewards those who earnestly seek him" (Heb. 11:6).

BLESSINGS AND THE RIGHTEOUS		REFERENCE NUMBERS

Bless

3:33	The Lord's curse is on the house of the wicked, but he **blesses** the home of the righteous.	1385
10:6	**Blessings** crown the head of the righteous, but violence overwhelms the mouth of the wicked.	1388
10:7	The memory of the righteous will be a **blessing,** but the name of the wicked will rot.	1388
11:11	Through the **blessing** of the upright a city is exalted, but by the mouth of the wicked it is destroyed.	1388
20:7	The righteous man leads a blameless life; **blessed** are his children after him.	897
28:20	A faithful man will be richly **blessed**, but one eager to get rich will not go unpunished.	1388

Favor

12:2	A good man obtains **favor** from the Lord, but the Lord condemns a crafty man.	8356
13:15	Good understanding wins **favor**, but the way of the unfaithful is hard.	2834

Good

11:27	He who seeks **good** finds goodwill, but evil comes to him who searches for it.	3202
14:14	The faithless will be fully repaid for their ways, and the **good** man rewarded for his.	3202
14:19	Evil men will bow down in the presence of the **good**, and the wicked at the gates of the righteous.	3202
14:22	Do not those who plot evil go astray? But those who plan what is **good** find love and faithfulness.	3202
15:3	The eyes of the Lord are everywhere, keeping watch on the wicked and the **good**.	3202
28:10	He who leads the upright along an evil path will fall into his own trap, but the blameless will receive a **good** inheritance.	3202

Goodwill

14:9	Fools mock at making amends for sin, but **goodwill** is found among the upright.	8356

Prayer

15:8	The Lord detests the sacrifice of the wicked, but the **prayer** of the upright pleases him.	9525
15:29	The Lord is far from the wicked but he hears the **prayer** of the righteous.	9525

Prosperity

13:21	Misfortune pursues the sinner, but **prosperity** is the reward of the righteous.	3202

		REFERENCE NUMBERS
16:20	Whoever gives heed to instruction **prospers**, and blessed is he who trusts in the LORD.	3202 + 5162
19:8	He who gets wisdom loves his own soul; he who cherishes understanding **prospers**.	3202 + 5162

Reward
| 11:18 | The wicked man earns deceptive wages, but he who sows righteousness reaps a sure **reward**. | 8512 |

BLESSINGS AND THE OBEDIENT

Bless
| 8:32 | "Now then, my sons, listen to me; **blessed** are those who keep my ways." | 897 |
| 8:34 | **Blessed** is the man who listens to me, watching daily at my doors, waiting at my doorway. | 897 |

Reward
| 13:13 | He who scorns instruction will pay for it, but he who respects a command is **rewarded**. | 8966 |

BLESSINGS AND FAMILY

Bless
| 5:18 | May your fountain be **blessed**, and may you rejoice in the wife of your youth. | 1385 |
| 31:28 | Her children arise and call her **blessed**; her husband also, and he praises her: | 897 |

Charm
| 31:30 | **Charm** is deceptive, and beauty is fleeting; but a woman who fears the LORD is to be praised. | 2834 |

Favor
| 18:22 | He who finds a wife finds what is good and receives **favor** from the LORD. | 8356 |

Good
| 13:22 | A **good** man leaves an inheritance for his children's children, but a sinner's wealth is stored up for the righteous. | 3202 |
| 31:12 | She brings him **good**, not harm, all the days of her life. | 3202 |

Profitable
| 31:18 | She sees that her trading is **profitable**, and her lamp does not go out at night. | 3202 |

BLESSINGS AND GIVING

Bless
| 11:26 | People curse the man who hoards grain, but **blessing** crowns him who is willing to sell. | 1388 |
| 22:9 | A generous man will himself be **blessed**, for he shares his food with the poor. | 1385 |

Favor
| 19:6 | Many curry **favor** with a ruler, and everyone is the friend of a man who gives gifts. | 2704 + 7156 |

Good
| 3:27 | Do not withhold **good** from those who deserve it, when it is in your power to act. | 3202 |

Reward
| 25:22 | In doing this, you will heap burning coals on his head, and the LORD will **reward** you. | 8966 |

BLESSINGS AND EFFECTIVE SPEECH

Good

13:2	From the fruit of his lips a man enjoys **good** things, but the un-faithful have a craving for violence.	3202
15:23	A man finds joy in giving an apt reply—and how **good** is a timely word!	3202
15:30	A cheerful look brings joy to the heart, and **good** news gives health to the bones.	3202
17:22	A cheerful heart is **good** medicine, but a crushed spirit dries up the bones.	3512
25:25	Like cold water to a weary soul is **good** news from a distant land.	3202

Kind

12:25	An anxious heart weighs a man down, but a **kind** word cheers him up.	3202

BLESSINGS AND WEALTH

Bless

10:22	The **blessing** of the Lord brings wealth, and he adds no trouble to it.	1388

Good

12:14	From the fruit of his lips a man is filled with **good** things as surely as the work of his hands rewards him.	3202

BLESSINGS AND JUSTICE

Bless

24:25	But it will go well with those who convict the guilty, and rich **blessing** will come upon them.	1388

Good

19:2	It is not **good** to have zeal without knowledge, nor to be hasty and miss the way.	3202
24:23	These also are sayings of the wise: To show partiality in judging is not **good**:	3202
28:21	To show partiality is not **good**—yet a man will do wrong for a piece of bread.	3202

CONTRASTS TO BLESSINGS

Does wickedness pay? In this present world sin sometimes appears to exact no price. Proverbs reminds us that evil's apparent cost-effectiveness is a deception. The truth? Wickedness is deceitful, dishonest, angry, and violent. In the end it steals away life itself. Only a fool forgets that God powerfully blesses trust and obedience, but curses rebellion and disobedience. Choices—right or wrong—exact consequences!

BLESSINGS CONTRASTED TO WICKEDNESS		REFERENCE NUMBERS
Cruel		
11:17	A kind man benefits himself, but a **cruel** man brings trouble on himself.	426
Evil		
11:27	He who seeks good finds goodwill, but **evil** comes to him who searches for it.	8288
14:22	Do not those who plot **evil** go astray? But those who plan what is good find love and faithfulness.	8273
17:13	If a man pays back **evil** for good, evil will never leave his house.	8288
28:10	He who leads the upright along an **evil** path will fall into his own trap, but the blameless will receive a good inheritance.	8288
Law		
28:9	If anyone turns a deaf ear to the **law**, even his prayers are detestable.	9368
Sinner		
13:21	Misfortune pursues the **sinner**, but prosperity is the reward of the righteous.	2629
13:22	A good man leaves an inheritance for his children's children, but a **sinner's** wealth is stored up for the righteous.	2627
Wicked		
3:33	The Lord's curse is on the house of the **wicked**, but he blesses the home of the righteous.	8401
10:6	Blessings crown the head of the righteous, but violence overwhelms the mouth of the **wicked**.	8401
10:7	The memory of the righteous will be a blessing, but the name of the **wicked** will rot.	8401
11:11	Through the blessing of the upright a city is exalted, but by the mouth of the **wicked** it is destroyed.	8401
11:18	The **wicked** man earns deceptive wages, but he who sows righteousness reaps a sure reward.	8401
11:23	The desire of the righteous ends only in good, but the hope of the **wicked** only in wrath.	8401
14:19	Evil men will bow down in the presence of the good, and the **wicked** at the gates of the righteous.	8401
15:8	The Lord detests the sacrifice of the **wicked**, but the prayer of the upright pleases him.	8401
15:29	The Lord is far from the **wicked** but he hears the prayer of the righteous.	8401
18:5	It is not good to be partial to the **wicked** or to deprive the innocent of justice.	8401
21:10	The **wicked** man craves evil; his neighbor gets no mercy from him.	8401

		REFERENCE NUMBERS
24:20	for the evil man has no future hope, and the lamp of the **wicked** will be snuffed out.	8401

Wrath

| 14:35 | A king delights in a wise servant, but a shameful servant incurs his **wrath**. | 6301 |

BLESSINGS CONTRASTED TO THE TONGUE

Curse

| 27:14 | If a man loudly blesses his neighbor early in the morning, it will be taken as a **curse**. | 7839 |
| 30:11 | "There are those who **curse** their fathers and do not bless their mothers" | 7837 |

Tongue

| 17:20 | A man of perverse heart does not prosper; he whose **tongue** is deceitful falls into trouble. | 4383 |

BLESSINGS CONTRASTED TO THE FOOL

Fool

| 14:9 | **Fools** mock at making amends for sin, but goodwill is found among the upright. | 211 |

Hasty

| 19:2 | It is not good to have zeal without knowledge, nor to be **hasty** and miss the way. | 237 + 928 + 8079 |

Scorn

| 13:13 | He who **scorns** instruction will pay for it, but he who respects a command is rewarded. | 996 |

BLESSINGS CONTRASTED TO ANGER

Rage

| 19:12 | A king's **rage** is like the roar of a lion, but his favor is like dew on the grass. | 2408 |

Violent

| 16:29 | A **violent** man entices his neighbor and leads him down a path that is not good. | 2805 |

BLESSINGS CONTRASTED TO UNFAITHFULNESS

Crafty

| 12:2 | A good man obtains favor from the LORD, but the LORD condemns a **crafty** man. | 4659 |

Unfaithful

13:2	From the fruit of his lips a man enjoys good things, but the **unfaithful** have a craving for violence.	953
13:15	Good understanding wins favor, but the way of the **unfaithful** is hard.	953
14:14	The **faithless** will be fully repaid for their ways, and the good man rewarded for his.	4213 + 6047

BLESSINGS CONTRASTED TO DECEIT

Dishonest

| 20:23 | The LORD detests differing weights, and **dishonest** scales do not please him. | 5327 |

THE BODY

In secular culture, the human body is either worshiped or debased. Wisdom recognizes our physical bodies as the Creator's gift to us. Each part of them can serve either evil or good. God desires both our bodies and our personalities to be healthy, thus Proverbs uses more than twenty different body parts to illustrate and apply its life-giving lessons.

THE BODY RELATED TO THE FAMILY AND A VIRTUOUS WIFE		REFERENCE NUMBERS

THE FAMILY

Eyes/Eyelids/Heart

6:4	Allow no sleep to your **eyes**, no slumber to your **eyelids**.	6524/6757
7:2	Keep my commands and you will live; guard my teachings as the apple of your **eye**.	6524
23:26	My son, give me your **heart** and let your **eyes** keep to my ways,	4213/6524
30:17	"The **eye** that mocks a father, that scorns obedience to a mother, will be pecked out by the ravens of the valley, will be eaten by the vultures."	6524

Hands

6:1	My son, if you have put up security for your neighbor, if you have struck **hands** in pledge for another,	4090
6:3	then do this, my son, to free yourself, since you have fallen into your neighbor's **hands**: Go and humble yourself; press your plea with your neighbor!	4090
6:5	Free yourself, like a gazelle from the **hand** of the hunter, like a bird from the snare of the fowler.	3338

A VIRTUOUS WIFE

Arms

31:17	She sets about her work vigorously; her **arms** are strong for her tasks.	2432

Bones

12:4	A wife of noble character is her husband's crown, but a disgraceful wife is like decay in his **bones**.	6795

Breasts/Bosom

5:19	A loving doe, a graceful deer—may her **breasts** satisfy you always, may you ever be captivated by her love.	1843
5:20	Why be captivated, my son, by an adulteress? Why embrace the **bosom** of another man's wife?	2668

Hands/Arms

14:1	The wise woman builds her house, but with her own **hands** the foolish one tears hers down.	3338
31:13	She selects wool and flax and works with eager **hands**.	4090
31:20	She opens her **arms** to the poor and extends her **hands** to the needy.	4090/3338

THE BODY RELATED TO DILIGENCE AND DISCIPLINE		

DILIGENCE

Lips/Hands

12:14	From the fruit of his **lips** a man is filled with good things as surely as the work of his **hands** rewards him.	7023/3338
12:24	Diligent **hands** will rule, but laziness ends in slave labor.	3338

REFERENCE
NUMBERS

DISCIPLINE

Ears

25:12   Like an earring of gold or an ornament of fine gold is a wise   265
man's rebuke to a listening **ear**.

Lips/Back

10:13   Wisdom is found on the **lips** of the discerning, but a rod is for   8557/1568
the **back** of him who lacks judgment.

19:29   Penalties are prepared for mockers, and beatings for the **backs**   1568
of fools.

26:3   A whip for the horse, a halter for the donkey, and a rod for the   1568
backs of fools!

Neck

29:1   A man who remains **stiff-necked** after many rebukes will sud-   6902 + 7996
denly be destroyed—without remedy.

THE BODY RELATED TO ANGER AND THE WICKED

ANGER

Nose

30:33   "For as churning the milk produces butter, and as twisting the   678
nose produces blood, so stirring up anger produces strife."

THE WICKED

Blood/Feet/Eyes/Tongue/Hands

1:11   If they say, "Come along with us; let's lie in wait for some-   1947
one's **blood**, let's waylay some harmless soul;"

1:16   for their **feet** rush into sin, they are swift to shed **blood**.   8079/1947

1:18   These men lie in wait for their own **blood**; they waylay only   1947
themselves!

6:17   haughty **eyes**, a lying **tongue**, **hands** that shed innocent **blood**,   6524/4383/
3338/1947

12:6   The words of the wicked lie in wait for **blood**, but the speech of   1947
the upright rescues them.

29:10   **Bloodthirsty** men hate a man of integrity and seek to kill the   1947
upright.

Eyes/Feet/Fingers/Lips

6:13   who winks with his **eye**, signals with his **feet** and motions with   6524/8079/
his **fingers**,   720

16:30   He who winks with his **eye** is plotting perversity; he who purses   6524/8557
his **lips** is bent on evil.

Heart/Feet

6:18   a **heart** that devises wicked schemes, **feet** that are quick to rush   4213/8079
into evil,

Stomach

13:25   The righteous eat to their hearts' content, but the **stomach** of   1061
the wicked goes hungry.

THE BODY AND THE TONGUE

Feet

29:5   Whoever flatters his neighbor is spreading a net for his **feet**.   7193

Lips/Tongue

17:4   A wicked man listens to evil **lips**; a liar pays attention to a mali-   8557/4383
cious **tongue**.

Mouth/Stomach/Lips

18:20   From the fruit of his **mouth** a man's **stomach** is filled; with the   7023/1061
harvest from his **lips** he is satisfied.   8557

Tongue/Bones

25:15   Through patience a ruler can be persuaded, and a gentle **tongue**   4383/1752
can break a **bone**.

THE BODY AND THE LORD

Eyes/Body/Bones/Ears

3:7-8   Do not be wise in your own **eyes**; fear the LORD and shun evil.   6524/9219/
[8] This will bring health to your **body** and nourishment to your   6795
bones.

15:3   The **eyes** of the LORD are everywhere, keeping watch on the   6524
wicked and the good.

20:12   **Ears** that hear and **eyes** that see—the LORD has made them   265/6524
both.

22:12   The **eyes** of the LORD keep watch over knowledge, but he frus-   6524
trates the words of the unfaithful.

29:13   The poor man and the oppressor have this in common: The   6524
LORD gives sight to the **eyes** of both.

Feet

3:26   for the LORD will be your confidence and will keep your **foot**   8079
from being snared.

Hands

30:4   Who has gone up to heaven and come down? Who has gathered   2908
up the wind in the hollow of his **hands**? Who has wrapped up the
waters in his cloak? Who has established all the ends of the earth?
What is his name, and the name of his son? Tell me if you know!

THE BODY AND IMMORALITY

Face

7:13-15   She took hold of him and kissed him and with a brazen **face** she   7156
said:
[14] "I have fellowship offerings at home; today I fulfilled
my vows. [15] So I came out to meet you; I looked for you and
have found you!"

Feet

5:5   Her **feet** go down to death; her steps lead straight to the grave.   8079

7:11   (She is loud and defiant, her **feet** never stay at home;   8079

Flesh/Body

5:11   At the end of your life you will groan, when your **flesh** and   1414/8638
body are spent.

Heart/Eyes

6:25   Do not lust in your **heart** after her beauty or let her captivate   4222/6757
you with her **eyes**,

30:12   those who are pure in their own **eyes** and yet are not cleansed of   6524
their filth;

Lap

6:27   Can a man scoop fire into his **lap** without his clothes being   2668
burned?

Liver

7:23   till an arrow pierces his **liver**, like a bird darting into a snare,   3879
little knowing it will cost him his life.

27

THE BODY AND HEALTH

Heart/Body/Bones

14:30	A **heart** at peace gives life to the **body**, but envy rots the **bones**.	4213/1414 6795
15:30	A cheerful look brings joy to the heart, and good news gives health to the **bones**.	6795
16:24	Pleasant words are a honeycomb, sweet to the soul and healing to the **bones**.	6795
17:22	A cheerful **heart** is good medicine, but a crushed spirit dries up the **bones**.	4213/1752

THE BODY RELATED TO THE POOR AND LAZINESS

THE POOR

Ears

21:13	If a man shuts his **ears** to the cry of the poor, he too will cry out and not be answered.	265

Eyes

28:27	He who gives to the poor will lack nothing, but he who closes his **eyes** to them receives many curses.	6524
29:13	The poor man and the oppressor have this in common: The LORD gives sight to the **eyes** of both.	6524

Hands

10:4	Lazy **hands** make a man poor, but diligent **hands** bring wealth.	4090/3338

Teeth/Jaws

30:14	those whose **teeth** are swords and whose **jaws** are set with knives to devour the poor from the earth, the needy from among mankind.	9094/5506

LAZINESS

Hands/Mouth

6:10	A little sleep, a little slumber, a little folding of the **hands** to rest—	3338
19:24	The sluggard buries his **hand** in the dish; he will not even bring it back to his **mouth**!	3338/7023
21:25	The sluggard's craving will be the death of him, because his **hands** refuse to work.	3338
26:15	The sluggard buries his **hand** in the dish; he is too lazy to bring it back to his **mouth**.	3338/7023

Teeth/Eyes/Feet

10:26	As vinegar to the **teeth** and smoke to the **eyes**, so is a sluggard to those who send him.	9094/6524
25:19	Like a bad **tooth** or a lame **foot** is reliance on the unfaithful in times of trouble.	9094/8079

THE BODY RELATED TO THE RIGHTEOUS AND WISDOM

THE RIGHTEOUS

Head/Mouth

10:6	Blessings crown the **head** of the righteous, but violence overwhelms the **mouth** of the wicked.	8031/7023

WISDOM

Ears/Heart

2:2	turning your **ear** to wisdom and applying your **heart** to understanding,	265/4213

		REFERENCE NUMBERS
18:15	The **heart** of the discerning acquires knowledge; the **ears** of the wise seek it out.	4213/265
23:12	Apply your **heart** to instruction and your **ears** to words of knowledge.	4213/265

Hands

| 3:16 | Long life is in her right **hand**; in her left **hand** are riches and honor. | NIH/NIH |

Head/Neck/Heart

1:9	They will be a garland to grace your **head** and a chain to adorn your **neck**.	8031/1738
3:21-22	My son, preserve sound judgment and discernment, do not let them out of your sight; [22] they will be life for you, an ornament to grace your **neck**.	1738
4:9	"She will set a garland of grace on your **head** and present you with a crown of splendor."	8031
6:20-21	My son, keep your father's commands and do not forsake your mother's teaching. [21] Bind them upon your **heart** forever; fasten them around your **neck**.	4213/1738

Sight

| 3:21 | My son, preserve sound judgment and discernment, do not let them out of your **sight**; | 6524 |

THE BODY AND INSTRUCTION

Ears

| 28:9 | If anyone turns a deaf **ear** to the law, even his prayers are detestable. | 265 |

Eyes/Feet/Foot

| 4:25-27 | Let your **eyes** look straight ahead, fix your gaze directly before you. [26] Make level paths for your **feet** and take only ways that are firm. [27] Do not swerve to the right or the left; keep your **foot** from evil. | 6524/8079/ 8079 |

Feet

1:15	my son, do not go along with them, do not set **foot** on their paths;	8079
3:26	for the LORD will be your confidence and will keep your **foot** from being snared.	8079
25:17	Seldom set **foot** in your neighbor's house—too much of you, and he will hate you.	8079

Fingers/Heart

| 7:3 | Bind them on your **fingers**; write them on the tablet of your **heart**. | 720/4213 |

Hands

| 1:24 | But since you rejected me when I called and no one gave heed when I stretched out my **hand**, | 3338 |
| 22:26 | Do not be a man who strikes **hands** in pledge or puts up security for debts; | 4090 |

Neck/Heart

| 3:3 | Let love and faithfulness never leave you; bind them around your **neck**, write them on the tablet of your **heart**. | 1738/4213 |

THE BODY AND AUTHORITIES

Eyes

| 20:8 | When a king sits on his throne to judge, he winnows out all evil with his **eyes**. | 6524 |

Hands
21:1   The king's heart is in the **hand** of the LORD; he directs it like a   3338
watercourse wherever he pleases.

Throat
23:1-2   When you sit to dine with a ruler, note well what is before you,   4350
[2] and put a knife to your **throat** if you are given to gluttony.

THE BODY RELATED TO THE FOOL AND THE PROUD

THE FOOL

Eyes
17:24   A discerning man keeps wisdom in view, but a fool's **eyes**   6524
wander to the ends of the earth.

Feet/Hand
26:6   Like cutting off one's **feet** or drinking violence is the sending   8079/3338
of a message by the **hand** of a fool.

Hands/Mouth
17:16   Of what use is money in the **hand** of a fool, since he has no   3338
desire to get wisdom?

17:18   A man lacking in judgment strikes **hands** in pledge and puts up   4090
security for his neighbor.

26:9   Like a thornbush in a drunkard's **hand** is a proverb in the   3338/7023
mouth of a fool.

Legs/Mouth
26:7   Like a lame man's **legs** that hang limp is a proverb in the   8797/7023
mouth of a fool.

THE PROUD

Eyes/Teeth/Jaws
30:13-14 those whose **eyes** are ever so haughty, whose glances are so 6524/9094/
disdainful; [14] those whose **teeth** are swords and whose **jaws**   5506
are set with knives to devour the poor from the earth, the needy
from among mankind.

Hand/Mouth
30:32   "If you have played the fool and exalted yourself, or if you   3338/7023
have planned evil, clap your **hand** over your **mouth**!"

Heart
16:5   The LORD detests all the proud of **heart**. Be sure of this: They   4213
will not go unpunished.

THE BODY AND GIVING

Head
25:21-22 If your enemy is hungry, give him food to eat; if he is thirsty,   8031
give him water to drink. [22] In doing this, you will heap burning coals on his **head**, and the LORD will reward you.

THE BODY AND ALCOHOL

Eyes
23:29   Who has woe? Who has sorrow? Who has strife? Who has   6524
complaints? Who has needless bruises? Who has bloodshot
eyes?

23:33   Your **eyes** will see strange sights and your mind imagine con-   6524
fusing things.

COMPARISONS AND CONTRASTS

Comparisons and contrasts are powerful teaching tools. Words such as *as, like, better,* and *but* transform abstract ideas into concrete, understandable principles for living. Throughout its pages Proverbs pictures the skillful life by means of these verbal object lessons, thus enabling truth to penetrate not only our minds, but our emotions and our wills as well.

COMPARISONS REGARDING THE WICKED		REFERENCE NUMBERS
As		
26:21	**As** charcoal to embers and **as** wood to fire, so is a quarrelsome man for kindling strife.	4006
But		
10:23	A fool finds pleasure in evil conduct, **but** a man of understanding delights in wisdom.	3983
10:25	When the storm has swept by, the wicked are gone, **but** the righteous stand firm forever.	3983
11:19	The truly righteous man attains life, **but** he who pursues evil goes to his death.	3983
Like		
1:12	let's swallow them alive, **like** the grave, and whole, **like** those who go down to the pit;	3869/3869
1:27	when calamity overtakes you **like** a storm, when disaster sweeps over you **like** a whirlwind, when distress and trouble overwhelm you.	3869/3869
4:19	But the way of the wicked is **like** deep darkness; they do not know what makes them stumble.	3869
16:27	A scoundrel plots evil, and his speech is **like** a scorching fire.	3869
17:14	Starting a quarrel is **like** breaching a dam; so drop the matter before a dispute breaks out.	NIH
25:26	**Like** a muddied spring or a polluted well is a righteous man who gives way to the wicked.	NIH
28:15	**Like** a roaring lion or a charging bear is a wicked man ruling over a helpless people.	NIH

COMPARISONS REGARDING THE RIGHTEOUS		
Better		
16:8	**Better** a little with righteousness than much gain with injustice.	3202
16:19	**Better** to be lowly in spirit and among the oppressed than to share plunder with the proud.	3202
19:22	What a man desires is unfailing love; **better** to be poor than a liar.	3202
28:6	**Better** a poor man whose walk is blameless than a rich man whose ways are perverse.	3202
But		
10:20	The tongue of the righteous is choice silver, **but** the heart of the wicked is of little value.	3983
11:20	The Lord detests men of perverse heart **but** he delights in those whose ways are blameless.	3983
11:28	Whoever trusts in his riches will fall, **but** the righteous will thrive like a green leaf.	3983
15:19	The way of the sluggard is blocked with thorns, **but** the path of the upright is a highway.	3983

		REFERENCE NUMBERS
21:8	The way of the guilty is devious, **but** the conduct of the innocent is upright.	3983
21:29	A wicked man puts up a bold front, **but** an upright man gives thought to his ways.	3983
28:1	The wicked man flees though no one pursues, **but** the righteous are as bold as a lion.	3983

Like

4:18	The path of the righteous is **like** the first gleam of dawn, shining ever brighter till the full light of day.	3869

COMPARISONS REGARDING GOD'S WORD

As

2:4	and if you look for it **as** for silver and search for it **as** for hidden treasure,	4006/4006
7:2	Keep my commands and you will live; guard my teachings **as** the apple of your eye.	4006

Better

16:16	How much **better** to get wisdom than gold, to choose understanding rather than silver!	3202

But

28:4	Those who forsake the law praise the wicked, **but** those who keep the law resist them.	3983

COMPARISONS REGARDING DISCIPLINE

As

3:12	because the LORD disciplines those he loves, **as** a father the son he delights in.	4006

Better

16:32	**Better** a patient man than a warrior, a man who controls his temper than one who takes a city.	3202
27:5	**Better** is open rebuke than hidden love.	3202

Like

25:28	**Like** a city whose walls are broken down is a man who lacks self-control.	NIH

COMPARISONS REGARDING IMMORALITY

As

5:3-4	For the lips of an adulteress drip honey, and her speech is smoother than oil; [4] but in the end she is bitter **as** gall, sharp **as** a double-edged sword.	4006

Like

6:5	Free yourself, **like** a gazelle from the hand of the hunter, **like** a bird from the snare of the fowler.	3869/3869
6:11	and poverty will come on you **like** a bandit and scarcity **like** an armed man.	3869/3869
7:22-23	All at once he followed her **like** an ox going to the slaughter, **like** a deer stepping into a noose [23] till an arrow pierces his liver, **like** a bird darting into a snare, little knowing it will cost him his life.	3869/3869
11:22	**Like** a gold ring in a pig's snout is a beautiful woman who shows no discretion.	NIH
23:28	**Like** a bandit she lies in wait, and multiplies the unfaithful among men.	3869

COMPARISONS REGARDING THE FAMILY		REFERENCE NUMBERS
Better		
15:17	**Better** a meal of vegetables where there is love than a fattened calf with hatred.	3202
17:1	**Better** a dry crust with peace and quiet than a house full of feasting, with strife.	3202
21:9	**Better** to live on a corner of the roof than share a house with a quarrelsome wife.	3202
21:19	**Better** to live in a desert than with a quarrelsome and ill-tempered wife.	3202
25:24	**Better** to live on a corner of the roof than share a house with a quarrelsome wife.	3202
Like		
12:4	A wife of noble character is her husband's crown, but a disgraceful wife is **like** decay in his bones.	3869
27:15-16	A quarrelsome wife is **like** a constant dripping on a rainy day; [16] restraining her is **like** restraining the wind or grasping oil with the hand.	8750/NIH
31:14	She is **like** the merchant ships, bringing her food from afar.	3869

COMPARISONS REGARDING GOD

Better		
15:16	**Better** a little with the fear of the LORD than great wealth with turmoil.	3202

COMPARISONS REGARDING LAZINESS

As		
10:26	**As** vinegar to the teeth and smoke to the eyes, so is a sluggard to those who send him.	4006
26:14	**As** a door turns on its hinges, so a sluggard turns on his bed.	4006
But		
15:19	The way of the sluggard is blocked with thorns, **but** the path of the upright is a highway.	3983
Like		
24:34	and poverty will come on you **like** a bandit and scarcity **like** an armed man.	NIH

COMPARISONS REGARDING AUTHORITIES

Better		
25:6-7	Do not exalt yourself in the king's presence, and do not claim a place among great men; [7] it is **better** for him to say to you, "Come up here," than for him to humiliate you before a nobleman.	3202
Like		
16:15	When a king's face brightens, it means life; his favor is **like** a rain cloud in spring.	3869
19:12	A king's rage is **like** the roar of a lion, but his favor is **like** dew on the grass.	3869/3869
20:2	A king's wrath is **like** the roar of a lion; he who angers him forfeits his life.	3869
21:1	The king's heart is in the hand of the LORD; he directs it **like** a watercourse wherever he pleases.	NIH

		REFERENCE NUMBERS
COMPARISONS REGARDING THE TONGUE		

Better

19:1   **Better** a poor man whose walk is blameless than a fool whose lips are perverse.   3202

But

18:4   The words of a man's mouth are deep waters, **but** the fountain of wisdom is a bubbling brook.   3983

Like

12:18   Reckless words pierce **like** a sword, but the tongue of the wise brings healing.   3869

18:8   The words of a gossip are **like** choice morsels; they go down to a man's inmost parts.   3869

25:11-12   A word aptly spoken is **like** apples of gold in settings of silver. [12] **Like** an earring of gold or an ornament of fine gold is a wise man's rebuke to a listening ear.   NIH/NIH

25:14   **Like** clouds and wind without rain is a man who boasts of gifts he does not give.   NIH

26:2   **Like** a fluttering sparrow or a darting swallow, an undeserved curse does not come to rest.   3869

26:22-23   The words of a gossip are **like** choice morsels; they go down to a man's inmost parts. [23] **Like** a coating of glaze over earthenware are fervent lips with an evil heart.   3869/3869

COMPARISONS REGARDING THE POOR

Like

28:3   A ruler who oppresses the poor is **like** a driving rain that leaves no crops.   NIH

COMPARISONS REGARDING ENCOURAGEMENT

But

17:22   A cheerful heart is good medicine, **but** a crushed spirit dries up the bones.   3983

27:21   The crucible for silver and the furnace for gold, **but** man is tested by the praise he receives.   3983

Like

25:13   **Like** the coolness of snow at harvest time is a trustworthy messenger to those who send him; he refreshes the spirit of his masters.   3869

25:20   **Like** one who takes away a garment on a cold day, or **like** vinegar poured on soda, is one who sings songs to a heavy heart.   NIH/NIH

25:25   **Like** cold water to a weary soul is good news from a distant land.   NIH

COMPARISONS REGARDING THE FOOL

As

26:11   **As** a dog returns to its vomit, so a fool repeats his folly.   4006

Like

26:1   **Like** snow in summer or rain in harvest, honor is not fitting for a fool.   3869

26:4   Do not answer a fool according to his folly, or you will be **like** him yourself.   8750

26:8-9   **Like** tying a stone in a sling is the giving of honor to a fool. [9] **Like** a thornbush in a drunkard's hand is a proverb in the mouth of a fool.   3869/NIH

COMPARISONS REGARDING FRIENDSHIPS

Better

27:10   Do not forsake your friend and the friend of your father, and do   3202
         not go to your brother's house when disaster strikes you—**bet-**
         ter a neighbor nearby than a brother far away.

But

20:5   The purposes of a man's heart are deep waters, **but** a man of   3983
         understanding draws them out.

Like

18:19   An offended brother is more unyielding than a fortified city,   3869
         and disputes are **like** the barred gates of a citadel.

CONTENTMENT

Satisfaction, peace, and safety—these are the qualities of the contented life, and Proverbs tells us the path to take to achieve them. Paul followed this wise path and was able to say, "I have learned to be content whatever the circumstances" (Phil. 4:11*b*). Jesus alone can give us the faithfulness, righteousness, truth and humility that generate this contentedness. In a materialistic society that is constantly griping—"we can't get no satisfaction"—believers can live filled and satisfied with God. "Be content with what you have, because God has said, 'Never will I leave you; never will I forsake you'" (Heb. 13:5*b*).

CONTENTMENT AND SATISFACTION		REFERENCE NUMBERS
Abundant		
12:11	He who works his land will have **abundant** food, but he who chases fantasies lacks judgment.	8425
Bread		
30:8-9	Keep falsehood and lies far from me; give me neither poverty nor riches, but give me only my daily **bread.** [9] Otherwise, I may have too much and disown you and say, 'Who is the LORD?' Or I may become poor and steal, and so dishonor the name of my God.	2976 + 4312
Content		
19:23	The fear of the LORD leads to life: Then one rests **content**, untouched by trouble.	8428
Dwelling		
24:15-16	Do not lie in wait like an outlaw against a righteous man's house, do not raid his **dwelling** place; [16] for though a righteous man falls seven times, he rises again, but the wicked are brought down by calamity.	8070
Good		
13:2	From the fruit of his lips a man enjoys **good** things, but the unfaithful have a craving for violence.	3202
Paths		
4:26-27	Make level **paths** for your feet and take only ways that are firm. [27] Do not swerve to the right or the left; keep your foot from evil.	5047
Peace		
29:17	Discipline your son, and he will give you **peace**; he will bring delight to your soul.	5663
Pleasing		
22:18	for it is **pleasing** when you keep them in your heart and have all of them ready on your lips.	5833
Rewarded		
12:14	From the fruit of his lips a man is filled with good things as surely as the work of his hands **rewards** him.	8740
14:14	The faithless will be fully repaid for their ways, and the good man **rewarded** for his.	NIH
Spare		
20:13	Do not love sleep or you will grow poor; stay awake and you will have food to **spare**.	8425

CONTENTMENT AND PROTECTION		REFERENCE NUMBERS

Deliver

20:22   Do not say, "I'll pay you back for this wrong!" Wait for the LORD, and he will **deliver** you.   3828

Fear/Lord

16:6   Through love and faithfulness sin is atoned for; through the **fear of the LORD** a man avoids evil.   3711/3378

Grace

1:8-9   Listen, my son, to your father's instruction and do not forsake your mother's teaching. [9] They will be a garland to **grace** your head and a chain to adorn your neck.   2834

Harm

12:21   No **harm** befalls the righteous, but the wicked have their fill of trouble.   224

Life

3:21-22   My son, preserve sound judgment and discernment, do not let them out of your sight; [22] they will be **life** for you, an ornament to grace your neck.   2644

Safety

1:33   "but whoever listens to me will live in **safety** and be at ease, without fear of harm."   8435

18:10   The name of the LORD is a strong tower; the righteous run to it and are **safe.**   8435

28:26   He who trusts in himself is a fool, but he who walks in wisdom is kept **safe.**   4880

29:25   Fear of man will prove to be a snare, but whoever trusts in the LORD is kept **safe.**   8435

Shield

30:5   "Every word of God is flawless; he is a **shield** to those who take refuge in him."   4482

Untouched

19:23   The fear of the LORD leads to life: Then one rests content, **untouched** by trouble.   1153 + 7212

Victory

11:14   For lack of guidance a nation falls, but many advisers make **victory** sure.   9591

21:31   The horse is made ready for the day of battle, but **victory** rests with the LORD.   9591

24:6   for waging war you need guidance, and for **victory** many advisers.   9591

CONTENTMENT RELATED TO FAITHFULNESS AND THE RIGHTEOUS

FAITHFULNESS

Faithful

20:6   Many a man claims to have unfailing love, but a **faithful** man who can find?   574

28:20   A **faithful** man will be richly blessed, but one eager to get rich will not go unpunished.   575

Trusted

27:6   Wounds from a friend can be **trusted**, but an enemy multiplies kisses.   586

Trustworthy

11:13   A gossip betrays a confidence, but a **trustworthy** man keeps a secret.   586 + 8120

REFERENCE
NUMBERS

| 13:17 | A wicked messenger falls into trouble, but a **trustworthy** envoy brings healing. | 574 |

| 25:13 | Like the coolness of snow at harvest time is a **trustworthy** messenger to those who send him; he refreshes the spirit of his masters. | 586 |

Truthful

| 14:5 | A **truthful** witness does not deceive, but a false witness pours out lies. | 574 |

THE RIGHTEOUS

Law

| 28:4 | Those who forsake the **law** praise the wicked, but those who keep the **law** resist them. | 9368/9368 |

Pure

| 15:26 | The LORD detests the thoughts of the wicked, but those of the **pure** are pleasing to him. | 3196 |

Righteous

| 10:21 | The lips of the **righteous** nourish many, but fools die for lack of judgment. | 7404 |

| 11:30-31 | The fruit of the **righteous** is a tree of life, and he who wins souls is wise. [31] If the **righteous** receive their due on earth, how much more the ungodly and the sinner! | 7404 |

| 12:3 | A man cannot be established through wickedness, but the **righteous** cannot be uprooted. | 7404 |

| 12:7 | Wicked men are overthrown and are no more, but the house of the **righteous** stands firm. | 7404 |

| 12:12 | The wicked desire the plunder of evil men, but the root of the **righteous** flourishes. | 7404 |

Upright

| 2:21 | For the **upright** will live in the land, and the blameless will remain in it; | 3838 |

CONTENTMENT RELATED TO TRUTH AND WISDOM

TRUTH

Truthful

| 12:19 | **Truthful** lips endure forever, but a lying tongue lasts only a moment. | 622 |

WISDOM

Grace

| 4:9 | "She will set a garland of **grace** on your head and present you with a crown of splendor." | 2834 |

Integrity

| 10:9 | The man of **integrity** walks securely, but he who takes crooked paths will be found out. | 9448 |

Pleasant

| 3:17 | Her ways are **pleasant** ways, and all her paths are peace. | 5840 |

Wisdom

| 14:33 | **Wisdom** reposes in the heart of the discerning and even among fools she lets herself be known. | 2683 |

| 24:3-4 | By **wisdom** a house is built, and through understanding it is established; [4] through knowledge its rooms are filled with rare and beautiful treasures. | 2683 |

CONTENTMENT RELATED TO FINANCES AND FRIENDSHIPS

FINANCES

Filled

3:9-10   Honor the LORD with your wealth, with the firstfruits of all   4848
your crops; [10] then your barns will be **filled** to overflowing,
and your vats will brim over with new wine.

Wealth

8:20-21   I walk in the way of righteousness, along the paths of justice,   3780
[21] bestowing **wealth** on those who love me and making their
treasuries full.

Wise

21:20   In the house of the **wise** are stores of choice food and oil, but a   2682
foolish man devours all he has.

FRIENDSHIPS

Friend

27:6   Wounds from a **friend** can be trusted, but an enemy multiplies   170
kisses.

Trustfully

3:29   Do not plot harm against your neighbor, who lives **trustfully**   1055 + 4200
near you.

CONTENTMENT AND THE LORD

Trust

3:5-6   **Trust** in the LORD with all your heart and lean not on your own   1053
understanding; [6] in all your ways acknowledge him, and he
will make your paths straight.

16:20   Whoever gives heed to instruction prospers, and blessed is he   1053
who **trusts** in the LORD.

22:19   So that your **trust** may be in the LORD, I teach you today, even   4440
you.

28:25-26 A greedy man stirs up dissension, but he who **trusts** in the   1053/1053
LORD will prosper. [26] He who **trusts** in himself is a fool, but
he who walks in wisdom is kept safe.

29:25   Fear of man will prove to be a snare, but whoever **trusts** in the   1053
LORD is kept safe.

CONTENTMENT RELATED TO COUNSEL AND HUMILITY

COUNSEL

Advice

20:18   Make plans by seeking **advice;** if you wage war, obtain guid-   6783
ance.

Advisers

11:14   For lack of guidance a nation falls, but many **advisers** make   3446
victory sure.

15:22   Plans fail for lack of counsel, but with many **advisers** they suc-   3446
ceed.

24:6   for waging war you need guidance, and for victory many **ad-**   3446
visers.

Purpose

19:21   Many are the plans in a man's heart, but it is the Lord's **pur-**   6783
pose that prevails.

HUMILITY

Exalt

25:6   Do not **exalt** yourself in the king's presence, and do not claim a   2075
place among great men;

Humble

3:34   He mocks proud mockers but gives grace to the **humble.**   6705

Praise

27:2   Let another **praise** you, and not your own mouth; someone   2146
else, and not your own lips.

27:21   The crucible for silver and the furnace for gold, but man is test-   4545
ed by the **praise** he receives.

CONTENTMENT RELATED TO DISCIPLINE AND WORK

DISCIPLINE

Peace

29:17   Discipline your son, and he will give you **peace**; he will bring   5663
delight to your soul.

WORK

Commit

16:3   **Commit** to the LORD whatever you do, and your plans will suc-   1670
ceed.

Diligent

21:5   The plans of the **diligent** lead to profit as surely as haste leads   3026
to poverty.

Wages

10:16   The **wages** of the righteous bring them life, but the income of   7190
the wicked brings them punishment.

Work

12:11   He who **works** his land will have abundant food, but he who   6268
chases fantasies lacks judgment.

12:14   From the fruit of his lips a man is filled with good things as   1691
surely as the **work** of his hands rewards him.

22:29   Do you see a man skilled in his **work**? He will serve before   4856
kings; he will not serve before obscure men.

CONTENTMENT AND AUTHORITIES

Exalt

25:6-7   Do not **exalt** yourself in the king's presence, and do not claim a   2075
place among great men; [7] it is better for him to say to you,
"Come up here," than for him to humiliate you before a nobleman.

Honored

27:18   He who tends a fig tree will eat its fruit, and he who looks after   3877
his master will be **honored.**

Justice

29:4   By **justice** a king gives a country stability, but one who is   5477
greedy for bribes tears it down.

Life

28:16   A tyrannical ruler lacks judgment, but he who hates ill-gotten   799 + 3427
gain will enjoy a long **life.**

Order

28:2   When a country is rebellious, it has many rulers, but a man of   4026
understanding and knowledge maintains **order.**

Patience
25:15 Through **patience** a ruler can be persuaded, and a gentle tongue 678 + 802
can break a bone.

Pure
22:11 He who loves a **pure** heart and whose speech is gracious will 3196
have the king for his friend.

Righteousness
16:12 Kings detest wrongdoing, for a throne is established through 7407
righteousness.

25:5 remove the wicked from the king's presence, and his throne 7406
will be established through **righteousness**.

Secure
29:14 If a king judges the poor with fairness, his throne will always 3922
be **secure**.

Serve
22:29 Do you see a man skilled in his work? He will **serve** before 3656/3656
kings; he will not **serve** before obscure men.

CONTENTMENT AND THE TONGUE

Fruit
12:14 From the **fruit** of his lips a man is filled with good things as 7262
surely as the work of his hands rewards him.

13:2 From the **fruit** of his lips a man enjoys good things, but the un- 7262
faithful have a craving for violence.

18:21 The tongue has the power of life and death, and those who love 7262
it will eat its **fruit**.

Pleasant
16:24 **Pleasant** words are a honeycomb, sweet to the soul and healing 5840
to the bones.

Pleasing
22:17-18 Pay attention and listen to the sayings of the wise; apply your 5833
heart to what I teach, [18] or it is **pleasing** when you keep them
in your heart and have all of them ready on your lips.

Satisfied
18:20 From the fruit of his mouth a man's stomach is filled; with the 8425
harvest from his lips he is **satisfied**.

CONTENTMENT AND THE WIDOW

Widows
15:25 The LORD tears down the proud man's house but he keeps the 530
widow's boundaries intact.

CONTRASTS TO CONTENTMENT

Injustice
13:23 A poor man's field may produce abundant food, but **injustice** 4202 + 5477
sweeps it away.

Peace
29:9 If a wise man goes to court with a fool, the fool rages and 5739
scoffs, and there is no **peace**.

Quarrelsome
21:9 Better to live on a corner of the roof than share a house with a 4506
quarrelsome wife.

Satisfied

27:20   Death and Destruction are never **satisfied**, and neither are the   8425
eyes of man.

30:15-16 "The leech has two daughters. 'Give! Give!' they cry.   8425/8425
"There are three things that are never **satisfied**, four that
never say, 'Enough!': [16] the grave, the barren womb, land,
which is never **satisfied** with water, and fire, which never says,
'Enough!' "

DEATH

Our society naively believes the lie: "Go ahead! Break God's moral law! We are immune to divine punishment!" Proverbs confronts us with reality—God is the author of life and to turn away from Him, and His instruction, is to journey into the curse of death. The rejection of wisdom shortens life. Though patient and gentle, the righteous King will ultimately execute a just penalty against those who persist in their rebellion against His rule. The universality of death proves the universality of our treason against heaven. There is hope! The Savior came to "free those who all their lives were held in slavery by their fear of death" (Heb. 2:15).

		REFERENCE NUMBERS
DEATH AND REJECTING WISDOM		

Calamity

1:26-27	I in turn will laugh at your disaster; I will mock when **calamity** overtakes you—[27] when **calamity** overtakes you like a storm, when disaster sweeps over you like a whirlwind, when distress and trouble overwhelm you.	7065/7065
24:21-22	Fear the LORD and the king, my son, and do not join with the rebellious, [22] for those two will send sudden destruction upon them, and who knows what **calamities** they can bring?	7085

Death

5:23	He will **die** for lack of discipline, led astray by his own great folly.	4637
8:36	"But whoever fails to find me harms himself; all who hate me love **death**."	4638
14:12	There is a way that seems right to a man, but in the end it leads to **death**.	4638
16:25	There is a way that seems right to a man, but in the end it leads to **death**.	4638
19:16	He who obeys instructions guards his life, but he who is contemptuous of his ways will **die**.	4637
21:16	A man who strays from the path of understanding comes to rest in the company of the **dead**.	8327

Disaster

6:15	Therefore **disaster** will overtake him in an instant; he will suddenly be destroyed—without remedy.	369

DEATH AND THE FOOL

Destroy

1:32	For the waywardness of the simple will kill them, and the complacency of fools will **destroy** them;	6

Die

10:21	The lips of the righteous nourish many, but fools **die** for lack of judgment.	4637

Ruin

10:14	Wise men store up knowledge, but the mouth of a fool invites **ruin**.	4745

DEATH AND OPPRESSING THE POOR

Disaster

17:5	He who mocks the poor shows contempt for their Maker; whoever gloats over **disaster** will not go unpunished.	369

DEATH AND IMMORALITY

Death

2:18	For her house leads down to **death** and her paths to the spirits of the dead.	8327
5:5	Her feet go down to **death**; her steps lead straight to the grave.	4638
7:27	Her house is a highway to the grave, leading down to the chambers of **death**.	4638
9:18	But little do they know that the **dead** are there, that her guests are in the depths of the grave.	8327

DEATH AND THE WICKED

Death

11:7	When a wicked man **dies**, his hope perishes; all he expected from his power comes to nothing.	4638
11:19	The truly righteous man attains life, but he who pursues evil goes to his **death**.	4638
14:32	When calamity comes, the wicked are brought down, but even in **death** the righteous have a refuge.	4638

Destroy

11:3	The integrity of the upright guides them, but the unfaithful are **destroyed** by their duplicity.	8720
28:24	He who robs his father or mother and says, "It's not wrong"— he is partner to him who **destroys**.	5422

Destruction

15:11	Death and **Destruction** lie open before the LORD—how much more the hearts of men!	11
17:19	He who loves a quarrel loves sin; he who builds a high gate invites **destruction**.	8691
27:20	Death and **Destruction** are never satisfied, and neither are the eyes of man.	9

Ruin

10:29	The way of the LORD is a refuge for the righteous, but it is the **ruin** of those who do evil.	4745

DEATH AND THE TONGUE

Calamity

21:23	He who guards his mouth and his tongue keeps himself from **calamity**.	7650

Deadly

21:6	A fortune made by a lying tongue is a fleeting vapor and a **deadly** snare.	4638

Destroy

11:9	With his mouth the godless **destroys** his neighbor, but through knowledge the righteous escape.	8845

Ruin

13:3	He who guards his lips guards his life, but he who speaks rashly will come to **ruin**.	4745

Violence

24:1-2	Do not envy wicked men, do not desire their company; [2] for their hearts plot **violence**, and their lips talk about making trouble.	8719

DEATH AND PRIDE

Destruction
16:18   Pride goes before **destruction**, a haughty spirit before a fall.   8691
Downfall
18:12   Before his **downfall** a man's heart is proud, but humility comes   8691
before honor.

DEATH AND LACK OF DISCIPLINE

Death
15:10   Stern discipline awaits him who leaves the path; he who hates   4637
correction will **die**.
23:13   Do not withhold discipline from a child; if you punish him with   4637
the rod, he will not **die**.
24:11   Rescue those being led away to **death**; hold back those stagger-   4638
ing toward slaughter.
Destroy
29:1   A man who remains stiff-necked after many rebukes will sud-   8689
denly be **destroyed**—without remedy.

CONTRASTS TO DEATH

Life
14:27   The fear of the Lord is a fountain of **life**, turning a man from   2644
the snares of death.
19:16   He who obeys instructions guards his **life**, but he who is con-   5883
temptuous of his ways will die.
Righteousness
10:2   Ill-gotten treasures are of no value, but **righteousness** delivers   7407
from death.
11:4   Wealth is worthless in the day of wrath, but **righteousness** de-   7407
livers from death.
14:32   When calamity comes, the wicked are brought down, but even   7404
in death the **righteous** have a refuge.
Upright
11:3   The integrity of the **upright** guides them, but the unfaithful are   3938
destroyed by their duplicity.
Wise
13:14   The teaching of the **wise** is a fountain of life, turning a man   2682
from the snares of death.

DILIGENCE

Proverbs agrees with the amusing advertising slogan "We make money the old fashioned way! We earn it!" Diligence, not laziness; actions, not words; excellence, not mediocrity: these have been the counsel for success for centuries. Proverbs is God's inspired equivalent to today's popular motivational literature. The present "recreational" generation needs to hear that "daily bread" is still earned the "old-fashioned way"—by the sweat of our brows.

DILIGENCE AND WORK

		REFERENCE NUMBERS
Diligence		
10:4	Lazy hands make a man poor, but **diligent** hands bring wealth.	3026
12:27	The lazy man does not roast his game, but the **diligent** man prizes his possessions.	3026
13:4	The sluggard craves and gets nothing, but the desires of the **diligent** are fully satisfied.	3026
Labor		
16:26	The **laborer's** appetite works for him; his hunger drives him on.	6664
Wages		
10:16	The **wages** of the righteous bring them life, but the income of the wicked brings them punishment.	7190
Work		
14:23	All hard **work** brings a profit, but mere talk leads only to poverty.	6776
22:29	Do you see a man skilled in his **work**? He will serve before kings; he will not serve before obscure men.	4856
24:27	Finish your outdoor **work** and get your fields ready; after that, build your house.	4856
31:13	She selects wool and flax and **works** with eager hands.	6913
31:31	Give her the reward she has earned, and let her works **bring** her praise at the city gate.	5126

DILIGENCE AND DISCIPLINE

Guard		
4:23	Above all else, **guard** your heart, for it is the wellspring of life.	5915
Plans		
16:3	Commit to the Lord whatever you do, and your **plans** will succeed.	4742

DILIGENCE AND LEADERSHIP

Careful		
27:23	Be sure you know the condition of your flocks, give **careful** attention to your herds;	4213
Diligence		
12:24	**Diligent** hands will rule, but laziness ends in slave labor.	3026

DILIGENCE AND WEALTH

Money		
13:11	Dishonest **money** dwindles away, but he who gathers **money** little by little makes it grow.	2401/NIH

Profit

21:5   The plans of the diligent lead to **profit** as surely as haste leads   4639
to poverty.

Rich

23:4   Do not wear yourself out to get **rich**; have the wisdom to show   6947
restraint.

Toil

5:10   lest strangers feast on your wealth and your **toil** enrich another   6776
man's house.

Wages

11:18   The wicked man earns deceptive **wages**, but he who sows righ-   7190
teousness reaps a sure reward.

DISCIPLINE

Mention *discipline* and it conjures up images of "spankings," "groundings," and "demerits." Though Proverbs does confront us with the need for the "rod of correction" (not to be confused with child abuse), *punishment* is hardly what the wise teacher means by discipline. *Discipline*—coaching and training the young in the skills of life, answering their "Why" questions about right and wrong—this is discipline in Solomon's school. God is the ultimate Father and Teacher. He never spoils, but always loves and disciplines for our good.

DISCIPLINE AND THE LORD

		REFERENCE NUMBERS

Discipline/Correction

3:11   My son, do not despise the Lord's **discipline** and do not resent his rebuke,   4592

6:23   For these commands are a lamp, this teaching is a light, and the **corrections** of **discipline** are the way to life,   9350/4592

Rebuke

1:23   If you had responded to my **rebuke**, I would have poured out my heart to you and made my thoughts known to you.   9350

1:25   since you ignored all my advice and would not accept my **rebuke**,   9350

1:30   since they would not accept my advice and spurned my **rebuke**,   9350

30:6   Do not add to his words, or he will **rebuke** you and prove you a liar.   3519

DISCIPLINE AND CHILDREN

Contempt

27:11   Be wise, my son, and bring joy to my heart; then I can answer anyone who treats me with **contempt**.   3070

Discipline/Correction

13:24   He who spares the rod hates his son, but he who loves him is careful to **discipline** him.   4592

15:5   A fool spurns his father's **discipline**, but whoever heeds **correction** shows prudence.   9350/4592

29:15   The rod of **correction** imparts wisdom, but a child left to himself disgraces his mother.   9350/4592

Disgrace

19:26   He who robs his father and drives out his mother is a son who brings shame and **disgrace**.   2917

Rebuke

13:1   A wise son heeds his father's instruction, but a mocker does not listen to **rebuke**.   1722

Train

22:6   **Train** a child in the way he should go, and when he is old he will not turn from it.   2852

DISCIPLINE AND BLESSINGS

Beatings

20:30   Blows and wounds cleanse away evil, and **beatings** purge the inmost being.   4804

Convict
24:25   But it will go well with those who **convict** the guilty, and rich   3519
        blessing will come upon them.
Discipline/Correction
10:17   He who heeds **discipline** shows the way to life, but whoever   9350/4592
        ignores **correction** leads others astray.
13:18   He who ignores **discipline** comes to poverty and shame, but   9350/4592
        whoever heeds **correction** is honored.
15:32   He who ignores **discipline** despises himself, but whoever heeds   9350/4592
        correction gains understanding.
Punish
21:11   When a mocker is **punished**, the simple gain wisdom; when a   6740
        wise man is instructed, he gets knowledge.
Rebuke
28:23   He who **rebukes** a man will in the end gain more favor than he   3519
        who has a flattering tongue.

DISCIPLINE AND PUNISHMENT

Contempt
14:31   He who oppresses the poor shows **contempt** for their Maker,   3070
        but whoever is kind to the needy honors God.
17:5   He who mocks the poor shows **contempt** for their Maker; who-   3070
        ever gloats over disaster will not go unpunished.
Discipline/Correction
5:12   You will say, "How I hated **discipline**! How my heart spurned   4592/9350
        correction!
10:17   He who heeds **discipline** shows the way to life, but whoever   4592/9350
        ignores **correction** leads others astray.
12:1   Whoever loves **discipline** loves knowledge, but he who hates   4592/9350
        correction is stupid.
13:18   He who ignores **discipline** comes to poverty and shame, but   4592/9350
        whoever heeds **correction** is honored.
15:10   Stern **discipline** awaits him who leaves the path; he who hates   4592/9350
        correction will die.
15:32   He who ignores **discipline** despises himself, but whoever heeds   4592/9350
        correction gains understanding.
Disgrace
14:34   Righteousness exalts a nation, but sin is a **disgrace** to any peo-   2875
        ple.
18:3   When wickedness comes, so does contempt, and with shame   3075
        comes **disgrace**.
Penalty
19:19   A hot-tempered man must pay the **penalty**; if you rescue him,   6741
        you will have to do it again.
Rebuke
29:1   A man who remains stiff-necked after many **rebukes** will sud-   9350
        denly be destroyed—without remedy.
Shame
6:33   Blows and disgrace are his lot, and his **shame** will never be   3075
        wiped away;

DISCIPLINE AND THE MOCKER

Beatings

19:29   Penalties are prepared for mockers, and **beatings** for the backs of fools.   4547

Correction

15:12   A mocker resents **correction**; he will not consult the wise.   3519

Insults

22:10   Drive out the mocker, and out goes strife; quarrels and **insults** are ended.   7830

Punish

21:11   When a mocker is **punished**, the simple gain wisdom; when a wise man is instructed, he gets knowledge.   6740

Rebuke

9:7-8   "Whoever corrects a mocker invites insult; whoever **rebukes** a wicked man incurs abuse. [8] Do not **rebuke** a mocker or he will hate you; **rebuke** a wise man and he will love you.   3519/3519 3519

13:1   A wise son heeds his father's instruction, but a mocker does not listen to **rebuke**.   1722

19:25   Flog a mocker, and the simple will learn prudence; **rebuke** a discerning man, and he will gain knowledge.   3519

DISCIPLINE AND THE FOOL

Discipline/Correction

15:5   A fool spurns his father's **discipline**, but whoever heeds **correction** shows prudence.   4592/9350

Fool

19:29   Penalties are prepared for mockers, and beatings for the backs of **fools**.   4067

Rebuke

17:10   A **rebuke** impresses a man of discernment more than a hundred lashes a fool.   1722

DISCIPLINE AND THE WISE

Instructed

21:11   When a mocker is punished, the simple gain wisdom; when a wise man is **instructed**, he gets knowledge.   8505

Prudent

22:3   A **prudent** man sees danger and takes refuge, but the simple keep going and suffer for it.   6874

27:12   The **prudent** see danger and take refuge, but the simple keep going and suffer for it.   6874

Rebuke

9:8   Do not **rebuke** a mocker or he will hate you; **rebuke** a wise man and he will love you.   3519/3519

15:31   He who listens to a life-giving **rebuke** will be at home among the wise.   9350

17:10   A **rebuke** impresses a man of discernment more than a hundred lashes a fool.   1722

25:12   Like an earring of gold or an ornament of fine gold is a wise man's **rebuke** to a listening ear.   3519

27:5   Better is open **rebuke** than hidden love.   9350

FAMILY

Godliness, purity, prudence, discipline, trust—these values appear as old-fashioned as a Currier and Ives Christmas scene, yet they alone can cultivate the peace and security of a strong, healthy home. Proverbs is not nostalgically idealistic. It also cries out against the contemporary family killers—nagging, quarreling, rebellion, laziness, unfaithfulness, and indifference. The ultimate Father has given His philosophy of home building and child training in Proverbs. We could rediscover some old-fashioned warmth under our roofs—protection from the isolating cold—if we reapplied this wise teacher's handbook on family living.

THE FAMILY AND INSTRUCTION OF CHILDREN

		REFERENCE NUMBERS
Father		
1:8	Listen, my son, to your **father's** instruction and do not forsake your mother's teaching.	3
4:1	Listen, my sons, to a **father's** instruction; pay attention and gain understanding.	3
6:20	My son, keep your **father's** commands and do not forsake your mother's teaching.	3
13:1	A wise son heeds his **father's** instruction, but a mocker does not listen to rebuke.	3
Mother		
31:1	The sayings of King Lemuel—an oracle his **mother** taught him:	562
Son		
2:1	My **son**, if you accept my words and store up my commands within you,	1201
3:1	My **son**, do not forget my teaching, but keep my commands in your heart,	1201
3:21	My **son**, preserve sound judgment and discernment, do not let them out of your sight;	1201
4:10	Listen, my **son**, accept what I say, and the years of your life will be many.	1201
4:20	My **son**, pay attention to what I say; listen closely to my words.	1201
5:1	My **son**, pay attention to my wisdom, listen well to my words of insight,	1201
7:1	My **son**, keep my words and store up my commands within you.	1201
19:27	Stop listening to instruction, my **son**, and you will stray from the words of knowledge.	1201
23:26	My **son**, give me your heart and let your eyes keep to my ways,	1201
24:21	Fear the LORD and the king, my **son**, and do not join with the rebellious,	1201
Sons		
7:24	Now then, my **sons**, listen to me; pay attention to what I say.	1201
8:32	"Now then, my **sons**, listen to me; blessed are those who keep my ways."	1201

THE FAMILY AND THE WISE CHILD

Father		
10:1	The proverbs of Solomon: A wise son brings joy to his **father**, but a foolish son grief to his mother.	3

		REFERENCE NUMBERS
13:1	A wise son heeds his **father's** instruction, but a mocker does not listen to rebuke.	3
15:20	A wise son brings joy to his **father**, but a foolish man despises his mother.	3
23:25	May your **father** and mother be glad; may she who gave you birth rejoice!	3
29:3	A man who loves wisdom brings joy to his **father**, but a companion of prostitutes squanders his wealth.	3

Son

1:10	My **son**, if sinners entice you, do not give in to them.	1201
1:15	my **son**, do not go along with them, do not set foot on their paths;	1201
10:5	He who gathers crops in summer is a wise **son**, but he who sleeps during harvest is a disgraceful **son**.	1201/1201
23:15	My **son**, if your heart is wise, then my heart will be glad;	1201
23:19	Listen, my **son**, and be wise, and keep your heart on the right path.	1201
23:24	The father of a righteous man has great joy; he who has a wise **son** delights in him.	3528
27:11	Be wise, my **son**, and bring joy to my heart; then I can answer anyone who treats me with contempt.	1201
28:7	He who keeps the law is a discerning **son**, but a companion of gluttons disgraces his father.	1201

THE FAMILY AND THE FOOLISH CHILD

Father

15:5	A fool spurns his **father's** discipline, but whoever heeds correction shows prudence.	3
15:20	A wise son brings joy to his **father**, but a foolish man despises his mother.	3
17:21	To have a fool for a son brings grief; there is no joy for the **father** of a fool.	3
17:25	A foolish son brings grief to his **father** and bitterness to the one who bore him.	3
19:13	A foolish son is his **father's** ruin, and a quarrelsome wife is like a constant dripping.	3
19:26	He who robs his **father** and drives out his mother is a son who brings shame and disgrace.	3
20:20	If a man curses his **father** or mother, his lamp will be snuffed out in pitch darkness.	3
28:7	He who keeps the law is a discerning son, but a companion of gluttons disgraces his **father**.	3
28:24	He who robs his **father** or mother and says, "It's not wrong"— he is partner to him who destroys.	3
30:11	"There are those who curse their **fathers** and do not bless their mothers;"	3
30:17	"The eye that mocks a **father**, that scorns obedience to a mother, will be pecked out by the ravens of the valley, will be eaten by the vultures."	3

Mother

10:1	The proverbs of Solomon: A wise son brings joy to his father, but a foolish son grief to his **mother**.	562

52

REFERENCE
NUMBERS

Son

10:5   He who gathers crops in summer is a wise **son**, but he who   1201/1201
        sleeps during harvest is a disgraceful **son**.

17:2   A wise servant will rule over a disgraceful **son**, and will share   1201
        the inheritance as one of the brothers.

THE FAMILY AND THE HUSBAND

Children

13:22   A good man leaves an inheritance for his **children's children**,   1201/1201
        but a sinner's wealth is stored up for the righteous.

14:26   He who fears the LORD has a secure fortress, and for his **chil-**   1201
        dren it will be a refuge.

20:7   The righteous man leads a blameless life; blessed are his **chil-**   1201
        dren after him.

THE FAMILY AND PARENTAL RESPECT

Children

17:6   **Children's children** are a crown to the aged, and parents are   1201/1201
        the pride of their **children**.

31:28   Her **children** arise and call her blessed; her husband also, and   1201
        he praises her:

Father

23:22   Listen to your **father**, who gave you life, and do not despise   3
        your mother when she is old.

27:10   Do not forsake your friend and the friend of your **father**, and   3
        do not go to your brother's house when disaster strikes you—
        better a neighbor nearby than a brother far away.

THE FAMILY AND DISCIPLINE

Child

20:11   Even a **child** is known by his actions, by whether his conduct is   5853
        pure and right.

22:6   Train a **child** in the way he should go, and when he is old he   5853
        will not turn from it.

22:15   Folly is bound up in the heart of a **child**, but the rod of disci-   5853
        pline will drive it far from him.

23:13   Do not withhold discipline from a **child**; if you punish him with   5853
        the rod, he will not die.

29:15   The rod of correction imparts wisdom, but a **child** left to him-   5853
        self disgraces his mother.

Son

3:11-12 My **son**, do not despise the Lord's discipline and do not resent   1201/1201
        his rebuke, [12] because the LORD disciplines those he loves,
        as a father the **son** he delights in.

13:24   He who spares the rod hates his **son**, but he who loves him is   1201
        careful to discipline him.

19:18   Discipline your **son**, for in that there is hope; do not be a will-   1201
        ing party to his death.

29:17   Discipline your **son**, and he will give you peace; he will bring   1201
        delight to your soul.

		REFERENCE
THE FAMILY AND THE VIRTUOUS WIFE		NUMBERS

Husband

12:4	A wife of noble character is her **husband's** crown, but a disgraceful wife is like decay in his bones.	1251
31:11	Her **husband** has full confidence in her and lacks nothing of value.	1251
31:28	Her children arise and call her blessed; her **husband** also, and he praises her:	1251

Wife

5:18	May your fountain be blessed, and may you rejoice in the **wife** of your youth.	851
18:22	He who finds a **wife** finds what is good and receives favor from the LORD.	851
19:14	Houses and wealth are inherited from parents, but a prudent **wife** is from the LORD.	851

THE FAMILY AND THE CONTENTIOUS WIFE

Wife

12:4	A **wife** of noble character is her husband's crown, but a disgraceful **wife** is like decay in his bones.	851/NIH
19:13	A foolish son is his father's ruin, and a quarrelsome **wife** is like a constant dripping.	851

THE FAMILY AND ADULTERY

Wife

5:20	Why be captivated, my son, by an adulteress? Why embrace the bosom of another man's **wife**?	AIT
6:29	So is he who sleeps with another man's **wife**; no one who touches her will go unpunished.	851

FINANCES

Buy now! Borrow to cover the cost! Easy payment plan! The currency of our economy is the credit card. While the job holds firm the monthly payments seem easy, but when hard times strike, the easy money exacts a painful price. The wise individual slowly accumulates wealth and pays as he goes. He never forgets that the wealth of nations, and of individuals, is a gracious gift from the Lord. He remembers "Where your treasure is, there your heart will be also!" (Matt. 6:21). One's income tax return is an incisive diagnostic instrument that reveals his priorities. Hard work, savings, honesty, generosity—these traditional money tips remain the high finance God honors.

FINANCES AND BORROWING MONEY		REFERENCE NUMBERS
Borrower		
22:7	The rich rule over the poor, and the **borrower** is servant to the lender.	4278

FINANCES AND CO-SIGNING

Security		
6:1	My son, if you have put up **security** for your neighbor, if you have struck hands in pledge for another,	6842
11:15	He who puts up **security** for another will surely suffer, but whoever refuses to strike hands in pledge is safe.	6842
17:18	A man lacking in judgment strikes hands in pledge and puts up **security** for his neighbor.	6842 + 6859
20:16	Take the garment of one who puts up **security** for a stranger; hold it in pledge if he does it for a wayward woman.	6842
22:26	Do not be a man who strikes hands in pledge or puts up **security** for debts;	6842
27:13	Take the garment of one who puts up **security** for a stranger; hold it in pledge if he does it for a wayward woman.	6842

FINANCES AND HONESTY

Scales		
11:1	The Lord abhors dishonest **scales**, but accurate weights are his delight.	4404
16:11	Honest **scales** and balances are from the Lord; all the weights in the bag are of his making.	4404
20:23	The Lord detests differing weights, and dishonest **scales** do not please him.	4404
Weights		
20:10	Differing **weights** and differing measures— the Lord detests them both.	74 + 74 + 2256

FOOL

The proverbial fool might score a perfect 1600 on his Scholastic Aptitude Test; *foolishness* in Proverbs is a deficiency not in mental acumen but in practical moral discernment. Naivety, selfishness, sarcasm, anger,and complacency—these are the character traits that mark the F student in wisdom's school. Because such students' independent self-will refuses to listen to good advice, most will graduate to hardened, self-destructive criminality. A few will come to their senses, humble themselves, and escape the clutches of ethical stupidity. "He who has ears, let him hear!" (Matt. 11:15). The foolish man builds his house on the sand. But the wise man builds on the Rock.

		REFERENCE
THE FOOL AND REJECTION OF COUNSEL		NUMBERS

Fool

12:15	The way of a **fool** seems right to him, but a wise man listens to advice.	211
16:22	Understanding is a fountain of life to those who have it, but folly brings punishment to **fools**.	211
23:9	Do not speak to a **fool**, for he will scorn the wisdom of your words.	4067
26:4-5	Do not answer a **fool** according to his folly, or you will be like him yourself. [5] Answer a **fool** according to his folly, or he will be wise in his own eyes.	4067/4067
26:12	Do you see a man wise in his own eyes? There is more hope for a **fool** than for him.	4067
28:26	He who trusts in himself is a **fool**, but he who walks in wisdom is kept safe.	4067

THE FOOL IN RELATION TO REJECTION OF KNOWLEDGE AND WISDOM

Fool

1:7	The fear of the LORD is the beginning of knowledge, but **fools** despise wisdom and discipline.	211
1:22	"How long will you simple ones love your simple ways? How long will mockers delight in mockery and **fools** hate knowledge?"	4067
8:5	You who are simple, gain prudence; you who are **foolish**, gain understanding.	4067
10:21	The lips of the righteous nourish many, but **fools** die for lack of judgment.	211
13:16	Every prudent man acts out of knowledge, but a **fool** exposes his folly.	4067
14:7	Stay away from a **foolish** man, for you will not find knowledge on his lips.	4067
17:16	Of what use is money in the hand of a **fool**, since he has no desire to get wisdom?	4067
18:2	A **fool** finds no pleasure in understanding but delights in airing his own opinions.	4067
24:7	Wisdom is too high for a **fool**; in the assembly at the gate he has nothing to say.	211

Mocker

| 9:12 | "If you are wise, your wisdom will reward you; if you are a **mocker**, you alone will suffer." | 4329 |

		REFERENCE NUMBERS
14:6	The **mocker** seeks wisdom and finds none, but knowledge comes easily to the discerning.	4370

Simple
9:4-6	"Let all who are **simple** come in here!" she says to those who lack judgment. [5] "Come, eat my food and drink the wine I have mixed. [6] Leave your **simple** ways and you will live; walk in the way of understanding.	7343/7344

THE FOOL AND UNDEPENDABILITY

Fool
14:8	The wisdom of the prudent is to give thought to their ways, but the folly of **fools** is deception.	4067
26:6	Like cutting off one's feet or drinking violence is the sending of a message by the hand of a **fool**.	4067

THE FOOL AND LACK OF DISCERNMENT

Folly
9:13	The woman **folly** is loud; she is undisciplined and without knowledge.	4070
14:18	The simple inherit **folly**, but the prudent are crowned with knowledge.	222
15:21	**Folly** delights a man who lacks judgment, but a man of understanding keeps a straight course.	222
18:13	He who answers before listening—that is his **folly** and his shame.	222
24:9	The schemes of **folly** are sin, and men detest a mocker.	222

Fool
10:23	A **fool** finds pleasure in evil conduct, but a man of understanding delights in wisdom.	4067
14:1	The wise woman builds her house, but with her own hands the **foolish** one tears hers down.	222
26:7	Like a lame man's legs that hang limp is a proverb in the mouth of a **fool**.	4067
26:9	Like a thornbush in a drunkard's hand is a proverb in the mouth of a **fool**.	4067
28:26	He who trusts in himself is a **fool**, but he who walks in wisdom is kept safe.	4067
29:9	If a wise man goes to court with a **fool**, the **fool** rages and scoffs, and there is no peace.	211/NIH
30:32	"If you have played the **fool** and exalted yourself, or if you have planned evil, clap your hand over your mouth!"	5571

Simple
7:7	I saw among the **simple**, I noticed among the young men, a youth who lacked judgment.	7343
9:16	"Let all who are **simple** come in here!" she says to those who lack judgment.	7343
14:15	A **simple** man believes anything, but a prudent man gives thought to his steps.	7343
22:3	A prudent man sees danger and takes refuge, but the **simple** keep going and suffer for it.	7343
27:12	The prudent see danger and take refuge, but the **simple** keep going and suffer for it.	7343

THE FOOL AND A CARE-FREE LIFESTYLE

Folly

19:3   A man's own **folly** ruins his life, yet his heart rages against the   222
LORD.

Fool

1:32   For the waywardness of the simple will kill them, and the com-   4067
placency of **fools** will destroy them;

14:9   **Fools** mock at making amends for sin, but goodwill is found   211
among the upright.

14:24   The wealth of the wise is their crown, but the folly of **fools**   4067
yields folly.

17:24   A discerning man keeps wisdom in view, but a **fool's** eyes   4067
wander to the ends of the earth.

21:20   In the house of the wise are stores of choice food and oil, but a   4067
foolish man devours all he has.

26:11   As a dog returns to its vomit, so a **fool** repeats his folly.   4067

Mocker

21:24   The proud and arrogant man—"**Mocker**" is his name; he be-   4370
haves with overweening pride.

Simple

14:18   The **simple** inherit folly, but the prudent are crowned with   7343
knowledge.

THE FOOL AND A LACK OF SELF-CONTROL

Folly

14:29   A patient man has great understanding, but a quick-tempered   222
man displays **folly**.

Fool

14:16-17   A wise man fears the LORD and shuns evil, but a **fool** is hot-   4067/222
headed and reckless. [17] A quick-tempered man does **foolish**
things, and a crafty man is hated.

17:12   Better to meet a bear robbed of her cubs than a **fool** in his folly.   4067

20:3   It is to a man's honor to avoid strife, but every **fool** is quick to   211
quarrel.

27:3   Stone is heavy and sand a burden, but provocation by a **fool** is   211
heavier than both.

29:11   A **fool** gives full vent to his anger, but a wise man keeps him-   4067
self under control.

Mocker

29:8   **Mockers** stir up a city, but wise men turn away anger.   408 + 4371

THE FOOL AND SHAME

Fool

3:35   The wise inherit honor, but **fools** he holds up to shame.   4067

12:16   A **fool** shows his annoyance at once, but a prudent man over-   211
looks an insult.

13:16   Every prudent man acts out of knowledge, but a **fool** exposes   4067
his folly.

13:19   A longing fulfilled is sweet to the soul, but **fools** detest turning   4067
from evil.

26:1   Like snow in summer or rain in harvest, honor is not fitting for   4067
a **fool**.

26:8   Like tying a stone in a sling is the giving of honor to a **fool**.   4067

THE FOOL AND THE TONGUE

Fool

10:8	The wise in heart accept commands, but a chattering **fool** comes to ruin.	211
10:10	He who winks maliciously causes grief, and a chattering **fool** comes to ruin.	211
10:14	Wise men store up knowledge, but the mouth of a **fool** invites ruin.	211
10:18	He who conceals his hatred has lying lips, and whoever spreads slander is a **fool**.	4067
12:23	A prudent man keeps his knowledge to himself, but the heart of **fools** blurts out folly.	4067
14:3	A **fool's** talk brings a rod to his back, but the lips of the wise protect them.	211
15:2	The tongue of the wise commends knowledge, but the mouth of the **fool** gushes folly.	4067
15:7	The lips of the wise spread knowledge; not so the hearts of **fools**.	4067
15:14	The discerning heart seeks knowledge, but the mouth of a **fool** feeds on folly.	4067
17:7	Arrogant lips are unsuited to a **fool**—how much worse lying lips to a ruler!	5572
17:28	Even a **fool** is thought wise if he keeps silent, and discerning if he holds his tongue.	211
18:6-7	A **fool's** lips bring him strife, and his mouth invites a beating. [7] A **fool's** mouth is his undoing, and his lips are a snare to his soul.	4067/4067
19:1	Better a poor man whose walk is blameless than a **fool** whose lips are perverse.	4067
29:20	Do you see a man who speaks in haste? There is more hope for a **fool** than for him.	4067

THE FOOL AND SERVING THE WISE

Fool

11:29	He who brings trouble on his family will inherit only wind, and the **fool** will be servant to the wise.	211
14:33	Wisdom reposes in the heart of the discerning and even among **fools** she lets herself be known.	4067
19:10	It is not fitting for a **fool** to live in luxury— how much worse for a slave to rule over princes!	4067

THE FOOL AND BAD COMPANY

Fool

13:20	He who walks with the wise grows wise, but a companion of **fools** suffers harm.	4067

THE FOOL AND DISCIPLINE

Fool

14:3	A **fool's** talk brings a rod to his back, but the lips of the wise protect them.	211
17:10	A rebuke impresses a man of discernment more than a hundred lashes a **fool**.	4067
18:6	A **fool's** lips bring him strife, and his mouth invites a beating.	4067

26:3	A whip for the horse, a halter for the donkey, and a rod for the backs of **fools**!	4067
27:3	Stone is heavy and sand a burden, but provocation by a **fool** is heavier than both.	211

Mocker

9:7-8	"Whoever corrects a **mocker** invites insult; whoever rebukes a wicked man incurs abuse. [8] Do not rebuke a **mocker** or he will hate you; rebuke a wise man and he will love you."	4370/4370
13:1	A wise son heeds his father's instruction, but a **mocker** does not listen to rebuke.	4370
15:12	A **mocker** resents correction; he will not consult the wise.	4370
19:25	Flog a **mocker**, and the simple will learn prudence; rebuke a discerning man, and he will gain knowledge.	4370
19:29	Penalties are prepared for **mockers**, and beatings for the backs of fools.	4370
21:11	When a **mocker** is punished, the simple gain wisdom; when a wise man is instructed, he gets knowledge.	4370
22:10	Drive out the **mocker**, and out goes strife; quarrels and insults are ended.	4370

THE FOOL AND THE FAMILY

Folly

22:15	**Folly** is bound up in the heart of a child, but the rod of discipline will drive it far from him.	222

Fool

10:1	The proverbs of Solomon: A wise son brings joy to his father, but a **foolish** son grief to his mother.	4067
15:5	A **fool** spurns his father's discipline, but whoever heeds correction shows prudence.	211
15:20	A wise son brings joy to his father, but a **foolish** man despises his mother.	4067
17:21	To have a **fool** for a son brings grief; there is no joy for the father of a **fool**.	4067/5572
17:25	A **foolish** son brings grief to his father and bitterness to the one who bore him.	4067
19:13	A **foolish** son is his father's ruin, and a quarrelsome wife is like a constant dripping.	4067

FRIENDSHIPS

Good friendships nourish good living. Though a rare gem, there is a friend who sticks closer than a brother. Those who discover a "Jonathan" find trust, dependability, and protection. Even strong friendships, however, can be dissolved in the acid of bad financial entanglements, flattery, gossip, or slander. Friendship itself can become poisonous when the "in" group chosen is a gang of criminals. Proverbs agrees with the warning, "Bad company corrupts good manners!" (1 Cor. 15:33). Our choices in friendship expose the true core values controlling our lives deep inside.

		REFERENCE NUMBERS
FRIENDSHIPS AND ADMISSION OF FAULTS		
Another		
18:17	The first to present his case seems right, till **another** comes forward and questions him.	8276ˢ
Neighbor		
6:1-5	My son, if you have put up security for your **neighbor**, if you have struck hands in pledge for another, [2] if you have been trapped by what you said, ensnared by the words of your mouth, [3] then do this, my son, to free yourself, since you have fallen into your **neighbor's** hands: Go and humble yourself; press your plea with your **neighbor**! [4] Allow no sleep to your eyes, no slumber to your eyelids. [5] Free yourself, like a gazelle from the hand of the hunter, like a bird from the snare of the fowler.	8276/8276/ 8276
17:18	A man lacking in judgment strikes hands in pledge and puts up security for his **neighbor**.	8276
25:8	do not bring hastily to court, for what will you do in the end if your **neighbor** puts you to shame?	8276
FRIENDSHIPS AND UNCONDITIONAL LOVE		
Friend		
17:17	A **friend** loves at all times, and a brother is born for adversity.	8276
18:24	A man of many companions may come to ruin, but there is a **friend** who sticks closer than a brother.	170
27:10	Do not forsake your **friend** and the **friend** of your father, and do not go to your brother's house when disaster strikes you— better a neighbor nearby than a brother far away.	8276/8276
Friendship		
12:26	A righteous man is cautious in **friendship**, but the way of the wicked leads them astray.	8276
Neighbor		
3:29	Do not plot harm against your **neighbor**, who lives trustfully near you.	8276
FRIENDSHIPS AND THE TONGUE		
Friend		
16:28	A perverse man stirs up dissension, and a gossip separates close **friends**.	476
17:9	He who covers over an offense promotes love, but whoever repeats the matter separates close **friends**.	476
22:11	He who loves a pure heart and whose speech is gracious will have the king for his **friend**.	8276

REFERENCE
NUMBERS

Neighbor

11:9　　　With his mouth the godless destroys his **neighbor**, but through　8276
knowledge the righteous escape.

11:12　　A man who lacks judgment derides his **neighbor**, but a man of　8276
understanding holds his tongue.

24:28　　Do not testify against your **neighbor** without cause, or use your　8276
lips to deceive.

25:9　　　If you argue your case with a **neighbor**, do not betray another　8276
man's confidence,

25:18　　Like a club or a sword or a sharp arrow is the man who gives　8276
false testimony against his **neighbor**.

26:18-19　Like a madman shooting firebrands or deadly arrows [19] is a　8276
man who deceives his **neighbor** and says, "I was only jok-
ing!"

29:5　　　Whoever flatters his **neighbor** is spreading a net for his feet.　8276

FRIENDSHIPS AND WEALTH

Friend

14:20　　The poor are shunned even by their neighbors, but the rich have　170
many **friends**.

19:4　　　Wealth brings many **friends**, but a poor man's **friend** deserts　8276/8276
him.

19:6　　　Many curry favor with a ruler, and everyone is the **friend** of a　8276
man who gives gifts.

Neighbor

3:28　　　Do not say to your **neighbor**, "Come back later; I'll give it to-　8276
morrow"—when you now have it with you.

FRIENDSHIPS AND THE POOR

Friend

19:4　　　Wealth brings many **friends**, but a poor man's **friend** deserts　8276/8276
him.

19:7　　　A poor man is shunned by all his relatives—how much more do　5335
his **friends** avoid him! Though he pursues them with pleading,
they are nowhere to be found.

Needy

14:21　　He who despises his neighbor sins, but blessed is he who is　6705
kind to the **needy**.

Neighbors

14:20　　The poor are shunned even by their **neighbors**, but the rich　8276
have many friends.

FRIENDSHIPS AND BAD COMPANY

Friend

22:24　　Do not make **friends** with a hot-tempered man, do not asso-　8287
ciate with one easily angered,

Neighbor

16:29　　A violent man entices his **neighbor** and leads him down a path　8276
that is not good.

21:10　　The wicked man craves evil; his **neighbor** gets no mercy from　8276
him.

FRIENDSHIPS AND TIME

Neighbor

25:17   Seldom set foot in your **neighbor's** house—too much of you,   8276
and he will hate you.

GOD

What we believe about beginnings strongly determines the ending to our lives. Proverbs confronts us with the Creator and the King, who alone deserves worship. The wise individual makes three foundational commitments—to reverence Him, to trust Him, and to enjoy intimacy with Him. God is one judge who never needs a Senate hearing to determine who is telling the truth. He sees all and knows all. The Judge of all the earth will do right. The wicked will be cursed, but the righteous will enjoy His blessing forever because the Creator is not only a righteous Judge but also a tender Father to all who believe in His promise.

		REFERENCE NUMBERS
GOD IN RELATION TO KNOWLEDGE AND WISDOM		
Fear of the Lord		
1:7	The **fear of the Lord** is the beginning of knowledge, but fools despise wisdom and discipline.	3711/3378
1:29	Since they hated knowledge and did not choose to **fear the Lord**,	3711/3378
2:5-6	then you will understand the **fear of the Lord** and find the knowledge of God. [6] For the Lord gives wisdom, and from his mouth come knowledge and understanding.	3711/3378
9:10	"The **fear of the Lord** is the beginning of wisdom, and knowledge of the Holy One is understanding."	3711/3378
15:33	The **fear of the Lord** teaches a man wisdom, and humility comes before honor.	3711/3378
Lord		
14:16	A wise man fears the **Lord** and shuns evil, but a fool is hotheaded and reckless.	NIH
28:5	Evil men do not understand justice, but those who seek the **Lord** understand it fully.	3378
GOD AND HOLINESS		
Fear of the Lord		
3:7	Do not be wise in your own eyes; **fear the Lord** and shun evil.	3707/3378
8:13	To **fear the Lord** is to hate evil; I hate pride and arrogance, evil behavior and perverse speech.	3711/3378
14:2	He whose walk is upright **fears the Lord**, but he whose ways are devious despises him.	3707/3378
16:6	Through love and faithfulness sin is atoned for; through the **fear of the Lord** a man avoids evil.	3711/3378
23:17	Do not let your heart envy sinners, but always be zealous for the **fear of the Lord**.	3711/3378
Holy One		
9:10	knowledge of the **Holy One** is understanding.	7705
30:3	I have not learned wisdom, nor have I knowledge of the **Holy One**.	7705
Lord		
10:29	The way of the **Lord** is a refuge for the righteous, but it is the ruin of those who do evil.	3378
21:3	To do what is right and just is more acceptable to the **Lord** than sacrifice.	3378

GOD AND HONESTY

Lord

16:11   Honest scales and balances are from the **Lord**; all the weights   3378
in the bag are of his making.

GOD AND LIFE

Fear of the Lord

10:27   The **fear of the Lord** adds length to life, but the years of the   3711/3378
wicked are cut short.

14:27   The **fear of the Lord** is a fountain of life, turning a man from   3711/3378
the snares of death.

19:23   The **fear of the Lord** leads to life: Then one rests content, un-   3711/3378
touched by trouble.

22:4   Humility and the **fear of the Lord** bring wealth and honor and   3711/3378
life.

Lord

8:35   For whoever finds me finds life and receives favor from the   3378
Lord.

GOD AND BLESSINGS

Fear of the Lord

15:16   Better a little with the **fear of the Lord** than great wealth with   3711/3378
turmoil.

22:4   Humility and the **fear of the Lord** bring wealth and honor and   3711/3378
life.

31:30   Charm is deceptive, and beauty is fleeting; but a woman who   3710/3378
fears the Lord is to be praised.

God

3:4   Then you will win favor and a good name in the sight of **God**   466
and man.

Lord

3:32   for the **Lord** detests a perverse man but takes the upright into   3378
his confidence.

3:33   The **Lord's** curse is on the house of the wicked, but he blesses   3378
the home of the righteous.

10:3   The **Lord** does not let the righteous go hungry but he thwarts   3378
the craving of the wicked.

10:22   The blessing of the **Lord** brings wealth, and he adds no trouble   3378
to it.

12:2   A good man obtains favor from the **Lord**, but the **Lord** con-   3378/NIH
demns a crafty man.

16:3   Commit to the **Lord** whatever you do, and your plans will suc-   3378
ceed.

16:20   Whoever gives heed to instruction prospers, and blessed is he   3378
who trusts in the **Lord**.

18:22   He who finds a wife finds what is good and receives favor from   3378
the **Lord**.

19:14   Houses and wealth are inherited from parents, but a prudent   3378
wife is from the **Lord**.

19:17   He who is kind to the poor lends to the **Lord**, and he will re-   3378
ward him for what he has done.

25:21-22 If your enemy is hungry, give him food to eat; if he is thirsty,   3378
give him water to drink. [22] In doing this, you will heap burning coals on his head, and the **Lord** will reward you.

28:14	Blessed is the man who always fears the **Lord**, but he who hardens his heart falls into trouble.	NIH
28:25	A greedy man stirs up dissension, but he who trusts in the **Lord** will prosper.	3378
30:7	"Two things I ask of you, O **Lord**; do not refuse me before I die:"	NIH

GOD AND PROTECTION

Defender

23:11	their **Defender** is strong;	1457

Fear of the Lord

14:26	He who **fears the Lord** has a secure fortress, and for his children it will be a refuge.	3711/3378

God

30:5	"Every word of **God** is flawless; he is a shield to those who take refuge in him."	468

Lord

3:25-26	Have no fear of sudden disaster or of the ruin that overtakes the wicked, [26] for the **Lord** will be your confidence and will keep your foot from being snared.	3378
16:7	When a man's ways are pleasing to the **Lord**, he makes even his enemies live at peace with him.	3378
16:9	In his heart a man plans his course, but the **Lord** determines his steps.	3378
18:10	The name of the **Lord** is a strong tower; the righteous run to it and are safe.	3378

GOD AND TRUST

Lord

3:5-10	Trust in the **Lord** with all your heart and lean not on your own understanding; [6] in all your ways acknowledge him, and he will make your paths straight. [7] Do not be wise in your own eyes; fear the **Lord** and shun evil. [8] This will bring health to your body and nourishment to your bones. [9] Honor the **Lord** with your wealth, with the firstfruits of all your crops; [10] then your barns will be filled to overflowing, and your vats will brim over with new wine.	3378/3378/ 3378
16:1	To man belong the plans of the heart, but from the **Lord** comes the reply of the tongue.	3378
22:19	So that your trust may be in the **Lord**, I teach you today, even you.	3378

GOD AND OMNIPRESENCE

Lord

5:21	For a man's ways are in full view of the **Lord**, and he examines all his paths.	3378
15:3	The eyes of the **Lord** are everywhere, keeping watch on the wicked and the good.	3378
15:11	Death and Destruction lie open before the **Lord**—how much more the hearts of men!	3378
24:17-18	Do not gloat when your enemy falls; when he stumbles, do not let your heart rejoice, [18] or the **Lord** will see and disapprove and turn his wrath away from him.	3378

GOD AND CREATION

Lord

3:19	By wisdom the Lᴏʀᴅ laid the earth's foundations, by understanding he set the heavens in place;	3378
8:22	"The Lᴏʀᴅ brought me forth as the first of his works, before his deeds of old;"	3378
20:12	Ears that hear and eyes that see—the Lᴏʀᴅ has made them both.	3378
22:2	Rich and poor have this in common: The Lᴏʀᴅ is the Maker of them all.	3378
29:13	The poor man and the oppressor have this in common: The Lᴏʀᴅ gives sight to the eyes of both.	3378

Maker

14:31	He who oppresses the poor shows contempt for their **Maker**, but whoever is kind to the needy honors God.	6913
17:5	He who mocks the poor shows contempt for their **Maker**; whoever gloats over disaster will not go unpunished.	6913
22:2	The Lᴏʀᴅ is the **Maker** of them all.	6913

GOD AND SOVEREIGNTY

Lord

16:2	All a man's ways seem innocent to him, but motives are weighed by the Lᴏʀᴅ.	3378
16:4	The Lᴏʀᴅ works out everything for his own ends—even the wicked for a day of disaster.	3378
16:33	The lot is cast into the lap, but its every decision is from the Lᴏʀᴅ.	3378
17:3	The crucible for silver and the furnace for gold, but the Lᴏʀᴅ tests the heart.	3378
19:21	Many are the plans in a man's heart, but it is the Lᴏʀᴅ's purpose that prevails.	3378
20:24	A man's steps are directed by the Lᴏʀᴅ. How then can anyone understand his own way?	3378
20:27	The lamp of the Lᴏʀᴅ searches the spirit of a man ; it searches out his inmost being.	3378
21:1-2	The king's heart is in the hand of the Lᴏʀᴅ; he directs it like a watercourse wherever he pleases. [2] All a man's ways seem right to him, but the Lᴏʀᴅ weighs the heart.	3378
21:30	There is no wisdom, no insight, no plan that can succeed against the Lᴏʀᴅ.	3378
22:12	The eyes of the Lᴏʀᴅ keep watch over knowledge, but he frustrates the words of the unfaithful.	3378
29:26	Many seek an audience with a ruler, but it is from the Lᴏʀᴅ that man gets justice.	3378

GOD AND THE RIGHTEOUS

Lord

3:11-12	My son, do not despise the Lᴏʀᴅ's discipline and do not resent his rebuke, [12] because the Lᴏʀᴅ disciplines those he loves, as a father the son he delights in.	3378/3378
11:20	The Lᴏʀᴅ detests men of perverse heart but he delights in those whose ways are blameless.	3378
12:22	The Lᴏʀᴅ detests lying lips, but he delights in men who are truthful.	3378

		REFERENCE NUMBERS
15:8-9	The **Lord** detests the sacrifice of the wicked, but the prayer of the upright pleases him. [9] The **Lord** detests the way of the wicked but he loves those who pursue righteousness.	3378/3378
15:26	The **Lord** detests the thoughts of the wicked, but those of the pure are pleasing to him.	3378
15:29	The **Lord** is far from the wicked but he hears the prayer of the righteous.	3378

GOD AND THE WICKED

Lord

3:32-33	for the **Lord** detests a perverse man but takes the upright into his confidence. [33] The **Lord's** curse is on the house of the wicked, but he blesses the home of the righteous.	3378/3378
10:29	The way of the **Lord** is a refuge for the righteous, but it is the ruin of those who do evil.	3378
11:20	The **Lord** detests men of perverse heart but he delights in those whose ways are blameless.	3378
12:2	A good man obtains favor from the **Lord**, but the **Lord** condemns a crafty man.	3378/NIH
15:8-9	The **Lord** detests the sacrifice of the wicked, but the prayer of the upright pleases him. [9] The **Lord** detests the way of the wicked but he loves those who pursue righteousness.	3378/3378
15:25-26	The **Lord** tears down the proud man's house but he keeps the widow's boundaries intact. [26] The **Lord** detests the thoughts of the wicked, but those of the pure are pleasing to him.	3378/3378
15:29	The **Lord** is far from the wicked but he hears the prayer of the righteous.	3378
16:5	The **Lord** detests all the proud of heart. Be sure of this: They will not go unpunished.	3378
17:15	Acquitting the guilty and condemning the innocent—the **Lord** detests them both.	3378
19:3	A man's own folly ruins his life, yet his heart rages against the **Lord**.	3378
22:14	The mouth of an adulteress is a deep pit; he who is under the **Lord's** wrath will fall into it.	3378

Righteous One

21:12	The **Righteous One** takes note of the house of the wicked and brings the wicked to ruin.	7404

HATRED

Though righteous indignation is a healthy response to injustice, prolonged anger is the HIV virus of the soul. Bitterness can lie concealed behind smiling lips and friendly eyes, but it slowly breaks down one's immunity to vicious acts. We politely label it "only an annoyance" or "just bad temper," but Jesus identified anger as murder's blood kin. Like those infected with AIDS, many of hatred's victims remain unaware of their condition. The wise will ask God to search and destroy all malicious tendencies. They will release their private vendettas to His ultimate justice. The preventatives against bitterness can then express themselves—gentleness, patience, and love.

HATRED AND ANGER

		REFERENCE NUMBERS
Fury		
22:8	He who sows wickedness reaps trouble, and the rod of his **fury** will be destroyed.	6301
Quick-Tempered		
14:17	A **quick-tempered** man does foolish things, and a crafty man is hated.	678 + 7920
14:29	A patient man has great understanding, but a **quick-tempered** man displays folly.	7920 + 8120

HATRED AND THE TONGUE

Anger		
15:1	A gentle answer turns away wrath, but a harsh word stirs up **anger**.	678
25:23	As a north wind brings rain, so a sly tongue brings **angry** looks.	2404
Hate		
10:18	He who conceals his **hatred** has lying lips, and whoever spreads slander is a fool.	8534
13:5	The righteous **hate** what is false, but the wicked bring shame and disgrace.	8533

HATRED AND CONTENTIONS

Anger		
20:2	A king's wrath is like the roar of a lion; he who **angers** him forfeits his life.	6297
29:22	An **angry** man stirs up dissension, and a hot-tempered one commits many sins.	678
30:33	"For as churning the milk produces butter, and as twisting the nose produces blood, so stirring up **anger** produces strife."	678
Annoyance		
12:16	A fool shows his **annoyance** at once, but a prudent man overlooks an insult.	4088
Hate		
10:12	**Hatred** stirs up dissension, but love covers over all wrongs.	8534
15:17	Better a meal of vegetables where there is love than a fattened calf with **hatred**.	8534
Hot-Tempered		
15:18	A **hot-tempered** man stirs up dissension, but a patient man calms a quarrel.	2279

		REFERENCE NUMBERS
19:19	A **hot-tempered** man must pay the penalty; if you rescue him, you will have to do it again.	1524 + 2779

Mocker

| 29:8 | **Mockers** stir up a city, but wise men turn away anger. | 408 + 4371 |

Rage

| 29:9 | If a wise man goes to court with a fool, the fool **rages** and scoffs, and there is no peace. | 8074 |

Wrath

| 14:35 | A king delights in a wise servant, but a shameful servant incurs his **wrath**. | 6301 |

HATRED AND BAD COMPANY

Hot-Tempered

| 22:24 | Do not make friends with a **hot-tempered** man, do not associate with one easily angered. | 678 |

HATRED AND REJECTION OF DISCIPLINE

Hate

8:36	"But whoever fails to find me harms himself; all who **hate** me love death."	8533
9:8	Do not rebuke a mocker or he will **hate** you; rebuke a wise man and he will love you.	8533
12:1	Whoever loves discipline loves knowledge, but he who **hates** correction is stupid.	8533
13:24	He who spares the rod **hates** his son, but he who loves him is careful to discipline him.	8533
15:10	Stern discipline awaits him who leaves the path; he who **hates** correction will die.	8533

Wrath

| 24:17-18 | Do not gloat when your enemy falls; when he stumbles, do not let your heart rejoice, [18] or the LORD will see and disapprove and turn his **wrath** away from him. | 678 |

HATRED AND GREED

Greedy

| 15:27 | A **greedy** man brings trouble to his family, but he who hates bribes will live. | 1298 + 1299 |

Wrath

| 11:4 | Wealth is worthless in the day of **wrath**, but righteousness delivers from death. | 6301 |

CONTRASTS TO HATRED

Appease

| 16:14 | A king's wrath is a messenger of death, but a wise man will **appease** it. | 4105 |

Delights

| 14:35 | A king **delights** in a wise servant, but a shameful servant incurs his wrath. | 8356 |

Gentle

| 15:1 | A **gentle** answer turns away wrath, but a harsh word stirs up anger. | 8205 |

Gift
21:14	A **gift** given in secret soothes anger, and a bribe concealed in the cloak pacifies great wrath.	5508

Good
11:23	The desire of the righteous ends only in **good**, but the hope of the wicked only in wrath.	3202

Love
10:12	Hatred stirs up dissension, but **love** covers over all wrongs.	173
12:1	Whoever **loves** discipline **loves** knowledge, but he who hates correction is stupid.	170/170

Patient
14:29	A **patient** man has great understanding, but a quick-tempered man displays folly.	678 + 800
15:18	A hot-tempered man stirs up dissension, but a **patient** man calms a quarrel.	678 + 800
16:32	Better a **patient** man than a warrior, a man who controls his temper than one who takes a city.	678 + 800
19:11	A man's wisdom gives him **patience**; it is to his glory to overlook an offense.	678 + 799

Wise
29:8	Mockers stir up a city, but **wise** men turn away anger.	2682

HUMILITY

Pride is deaf to wisdom's advice, but humility eagerly listens. Whereas pride is pretentiously carrying out a personal advertising campaign, humility quietly seeks to meet the needs of others. Not concerned about "saving face," humility is smart enough to escape from bad obligations. Ironically, humility receives the final applause; for "God opposes the proud but gives grace to the humble" (James 4:6; cf. Prov. 3:34).

HUMILITY AND HONOR		REFERENCE NUMBERS
Honor		
4:7-8	Wisdom is supreme; therefore get wisdom. Though it cost all you have, get understanding. [8] Esteem her, and she will exalt you; embrace her, and she will **honor** you.	3877
15:33	The fear of the LORD teaches a man wisdom, and humility comes before **honor**.	3883
18:12	Before his downfall a man's heart is proud, but humility comes before **honor**.	3883
22:4	Humility and the fear of the LORD bring wealth and **honor** and life.	3883
29:23	A man's pride brings him low, but a man of lowly spirit gains **honor**.	3883
Lowly		
16:19	Better to be **lowly** in spirit and among the oppressed than to share plunder with the proud.	9166

HUMILITY AND BOASTING		
Honor		
25:27	It is not good to eat too much honey, nor is it honorable to seek one's own **honor**.	3883
Pretend		
12:9	Better to be a nobody and yet have a servant than **pretend** to be somebody and have no food.	3877

HUMILITY AND SELF-CONTROL		
Honor		
20:3	It is to a man's **honor** to avoid strife, but every fool is quick to quarrel.	3883
Respect		
11:16	A kindhearted woman gains **respect**, but ruthless men gain only wealth.	3883

HUMILITY AND INSTRUCTION		
Honor		
13:18	He who ignores discipline comes to poverty and shame, but whoever heeds correction is **honored**.	3877
Humility		
11:2	When pride comes, then comes disgrace, but with **humility** comes wisdom.	7560

HUMILITY AND THE POOR		
Honor		
14:31	He who oppresses the poor shows contempt for their Maker, but whoever is kind to the needy **honors** God.	3877

HUMILITY AND THE RIGHTEOUS

Honor

21:21   He who pursues righteousness and love finds life, prosperity   3883
and **honor**.

HUMILITY AND SERVING OTHERS

Honor

27:18   He who tends a fig tree will eat its fruit, and he who looks after   3877
his master will be **honored**.

Humble

6:1-5   My son, if you have put up security for your neighbor, if you   8346
have struck hands in pledge for another, [2] if you have been
trapped by what you said, ensnared by the words of your
mouth, [3] then do this, my son, to free yourself, since you
have fallen into your neighbor's hands: Go and **humble** yourself; press your plea with your neighbor! [4] Allow no sleep to
your eyes, no slumber to your eyelids. [5] Free yourself, like a
gazelle from the hand of the hunter, like a bird from the snare
of the fowler.

HUMILITY AND WISDOM

Honor

3:13-16   Blessed is the man who finds wisdom, the man who gains un-   3883
derstanding, [14] for she is more profitable than silver and
yields better returns than gold. [15] She is more precious than
rubies; nothing you desire can compare with her. [16] Long life
is in her right hand; in her left hand are riches and **honor**.

3:35   The wise inherit **honor**, but fools he holds up to shame.   3883

8:17-18   I love those who love me, and those who seek me find me. [18]   3883
With me are riches and **honor**, enduring wealth and prosperity.

IMMORALITY

Professional athletes, Hollywood stars, and business tycoons proclaim they can commit sex sin with impunity. The frequency of televised confessions of their HIV-positive condition proves that none of us, including celebrities, can escape the perils of immorality. Are condom ads the answer to the latest deadly sexually transmitted disease threatening the health of our nation? Obviously they decrease the probabilities, but why play sexual Russian roulette with your body? Proverbs realistically warns us against the consequences of immorality and celebrates the happiness found in obedience to the Designer's original sex blueprint.

IMMORALITY RELATED TO INSTRUCTION AND CONSEQUENCES	REFERENCE NUMBERS

Immoral/Wayward/Prositute/Adulteress/Adultery

6:20-35 My son, keep your father's commands and do not forsake your mother's teaching. [21] Bind them upon your heart forever; fasten them around your neck. [22] When you walk, they will guide you; when you sleep, they will watch over you; when you awake, they will speak to you. [23] For these commands are a lamp, this teaching is a light, and the corrections of discipline are the way to life, [24] keeping you from the **immoral** woman, from the smooth tongue of the **wayward** wife. [25] Do not lust in your heart after her beauty or let her captivate you with her eyes, [26] for the **prostitute** reduces you to a loaf of bread, and the **adulteress** preys upon your very life. [27] Can a man scoop fire into his lap without his clothes being burned? [28] Can a man walk on hot coals without his feet being scorched? [29] So is he who sleeps with another man's wife; no one who touches her will go unpunished.

[30] Men do not despise a thief if he steals to satisfy his hunger when he is starving. [31] Yet if he is caught, he must pay sevenfold, though it costs him all the wealth of his house. [32] But a man who commits **adultery** lacks judgment; whoever does so destroys himself. [33] Blows and disgrace are his lot, and his shame will never be wiped away; [34] for jealousy arouses a husband's fury, and he will show no mercy when he takes revenge. [35] He will not accept any compensation; he will refuse the bribe, however great it is.
8273/5799/
2390/
408 + 851/
5537

Prostitute

23:26-27 My son, give me your heart and let your eyes keep to my ways, [27] for a **prostitute** is a deep pit and a wayward wife is a narrow well.
2390

29:3 A man who loves wisdom brings joy to his father, but a companion of **prostitutes** squanders his wealth.
2390

Wayward

20:16 Take the garment of one who puts up security for a stranger; hold it in pledge if he does it for a **wayward** woman.
5799

27:13 Take the garment of one who puts up security for a stranger; hold it in pledge if he does it for a **wayward** woman.
5799

IMMORALITY AND CONSCIENCE

Adulteress

30:20 "This is the way of an **adulteress**: She eats and wipes her mouth and says, 'I've done nothing wrong.' "
5537

IMMORALITY AND THE TONGUE

Adulteress

2:16	It will save you also from the **adulteress**, from the wayward wife with her seductive words,	851 + 2424
5:3	For the lips of an **adulteress** drip honey, and her speech is smoother than oil;	2424
22:14	The mouth of an **adulteress** is a deep pit; he who is under the Lord's wrath will fall into it.	2424

Wayward

6:24	keeping you from the immoral woman, from the smooth tongue of the **wayward** wife.	5799
7:5	they will keep you from the adulteress, from the **wayward** wife with her seductive words.	5799

IMMORALITY AND THE FAMILY

Adulteress

5:1-23	My son, pay attention to my wisdom, listen well to my words of insight, [2] that you may maintain discretion and your lips may preserve knowledge. [3] For the lips of an **adulteress** drip honey, and her speech is smoother than oil; [4] but in the end she is bitter as gall, sharp as a double-edged sword. [5] Her feet go down to death; her steps lead straight to the grave. [6] She gives no thought to the way of life; her paths are crooked, but she knows it not.	2424/2424

[7] Now then, my sons, listen to me; do not turn aside from what I say. [8] Keep to a path far from her, do not go near the door of her house, [9] lest you give your best strength to others and your years to one who is cruel, [10] lest strangers feast on your wealth and your toil enrich another man's house. [11] At the end of your life you will groan, when your flesh and body are spent. [12] You will say, "How I hated discipline! How my heart spurned correction! [13] I would not obey my teachers or listen to my instructors. [14] I have come to the brink of utter ruin in the midst of the whole assembly."

[15] Drink water from your own cistern, running water from your own well. [16] Should your springs overflow in the streets, your streams of water in the public squares? [17] Let them be yours alone, never to be shared with strangers. [18] May your fountain be blessed, and may you rejoice in the wife of your youth. [19] A loving doe, a graceful deer—may her breasts satisfy you always, may you ever be captivated by her love. [20] Why be captivated, my son, by an **adulteress**? Why embrace the bosom of another man's wife?

[21] For a man's ways are in full view of the Lord, and he examines all his paths. [22] The evil deeds of a wicked man ensnare him; the cords of his sin hold him fast. [23] He will die for lack of discipline, led astray by his own great folly.

Prostitute

7:6-27	At the window of my house I looked out through the lattice. [7] I saw among the simple, I noticed among the young men, a youth who lacked judgment. [8] He was going down the street near her corner, walking along in the direction of her house [9] at twilight, as the day was fading, as the dark of night set in.	2390 + 408 + 851

[10] Then out came a woman to meet him, dressed like a **prostitute** and with crafty intent. [11] (She is loud and defiant, her feet never stay at home; [12] now in the street, now in the squares, at every corner she lurks.) [13] She took hold of him and kissed him and with a brazen face she said:

[14] "I have fellowship offerings at home; today I fulfilled my vows. [15] So I came out to meet you; I looked for you and have found you! [16] I have covered my bed with colored linens from Egypt. [17] I have perfumed my bed with myrrh, aloes and cinnamon. [18] Come, let's drink deep of love till morning; let's enjoy ourselves with love! [19] My husband is not at home; he has gone on a long journey. [20] He took his purse filled with money and will not be home till full moon."

[21] With persuasive words she led him astray; she seduced him with her smooth talk. [22] All at once he followed her like an ox going to the slaughter, like a deer stepping into a noose [23] till an arrow pierces his liver, like a bird darting into a snare, little knowing it will cost him his life.

[24] Now then, my sons, listen to me; pay attention to what I say. [25] Do not let your heart turn to her ways or stray into her paths. [26] Many are the victims she has brought down; her slain are a mighty throng. [27] Her house is a highway to the grave, leading down to the chambers of death.

Adulteress/Wayward

2:16-19   It will save you also from the **adulteress**, from the **wayward**   851 + 2424/
wife with her seductive words, [17] who has left the partner of   5799
her youth and ignored the covenant she made before God. [18]
For her house leads down to death and her paths to the spirits of
the dead. [19] None who go to her return or attain the paths of
life.

76

INSTRUCTION

Like a dad refusing to look at the instructions before putting together his child's toy, many of us try to put life together without following the Creator's design, but life is no toy. It makes sense to follow God's instructions. The wise individual is willing to begin as an apprentice in the trade of life, and learn to make skillful choices. When in doubt read the directions!

INSTRUCTION AND THE WISE MAN		REFERENCE NUMBERS
Advice		
12:15	The way of a fool seems right to him, but a wise man listens to **advice**.	6783
13:10	Pride only breeds quarrels, but wisdom is found in those who take **advice**.	3619
19:20	Listen to **advice** and accept instruction, and in the end you will be wise.	6783
Discipline		
10:17	He who heeds **discipline** shows the way to life, but whoever ignores correction leads others astray.	4592
12:1	Whoever loves **discipline** loves knowledge, but he who hates correction is stupid.	4592
23:23	Buy the truth and do not sell it; get wisdom, **discipline** and understanding.	4592
Guidance		
1:5	let the wise listen and add to their learning, and let the discerning get **guidance**—	9374
Instruction		
4:13	Hold on to **instruction**, do not let it go; guard it well, for it is your life.	4592
8:10	Choose my **instruction** instead of silver, knowledge rather than choice gold,	4592
8:33	Listen to my **instruction** and be wise; do not ignore it.	4592
21:11	When a mocker is punished, the simple gain wisdom; when a wise man is **instructed**, he gets knowledge.	8505
23:12	Apply your heart to **instruction** and your ears to words of knowledge.	4592
Instructions		
19:16	He who obeys **instructions** guards his life, but he who is contemptuous of his ways will die.	5184
Learning		
9:9	Instruct a wise man and he will be wiser still; teach a righteous man and he will add to his **learning**.	4375

INSTRUCTION AND PROPER JUDGMENT

Advisers		
11:14	For lack of guidance a nation falls, but many **advisers** make victory sure.	3446
24:6	for waging war you need guidance, and for victory many **advisers**.	3446
Counsel		
15:22	Plans fail for lack of **counsel**, but with many advisers they succeed.	6051

Instruction
16:20-23 Whoever gives heed to **instruction** prospers, and blessed is he   1821/4375/
who trusts in the LORD. [21] The wise in heart are called dis-   4375
cerning, and pleasant words promote **instruction**. [22] Understanding is a fountain of life to those who have it, but folly
brings punishment to fools. [23] A wise man's heart guides his
mouth, and his lips promote **instruction**.

Purposes
20:5   The **purposes** of a man's heart are deep waters, but a man of   6783
understanding draws them out.

INSTRUCTION AND THE SEEKING OF COUNSEL

Advice
19:20   Listen to **advice** and accept instruction, and in the end you will   6783
be wise.

20:18   Make plans by seeking **advice**; if you wage war, obtain guid-   6783
ance.

Counsel
27:9   Perfume and incense bring joy to the heart, and the pleasant-   6783
ness of one's friend springs from his earnest **counsel**.

INSTRUCTION AND THE REJECTING OF WISDOM

Advice
1:20-33 Wisdom calls aloud in the street, she raises her voice in the   6783/6783
public squares; [21] at the head of the noisy streets she cries
out, in the gateways of the city she makes her speech:
[22] "How long will you simple ones love your simple
ways? How long will mockers delight in mockery and fools
hate knowledge? [23] If you had responded to my rebuke, I
would have poured out my heart to you and made my thoughts
known to you. [24] But since you rejected me when I called
and no one gave heed when I stretched out my hand, [25] since
you ignored all my **advice** and would not accept my rebuke,
[26] I in turn will laugh at your disaster; I will mock when calamity overtakes you—[27] when calamity overtakes you like a
storm, when disaster sweeps over you like a whirlwind, when
distress and trouble overwhelm you.
[28] "Then they will call to me but I will not answer; they
will look for me but will not find me. [29] Since they hated
knowledge and did not choose to fear the LORD, [30] since they
would not accept my **advice** and spurned my rebuke, [31] they
will eat the fruit of their ways and be filled with the fruit of
their schemes. [32] For the waywardness of the simple will kill
them, and the complacency of fools will destroy them; [33] but
whoever listens to me will live in safety and be at ease, without
fear of harm."

INSTRUCTION AND THE LORD

Counsel
8:14   **Counsel** and sound judgment are mine; I have understanding   6783
and power.

Discipline
1:2-3   for attaining wisdom and **discipline**; for understanding words   4592/4592
of insight; [3] for acquiring a **disciplined** and prudent life, doing what is right and just and fair;

		REFERENCE NUMBERS
6:23	For these commands are a lamp, this teaching is a light, and the corrections of **discipline** are the way to life,	4592

Plans

19:21	Many are the **plans** in a man's heart, but it is the Lord's purpose that prevails.	4742
21:30	There is no wisdom, no insight, no **plan** that can succeed against the LORD.	6783

Teaches

15:33	The fear of the LORD **teaches** a man wisdom, and humility comes before honor.	4592

INSTRUCTION AND THE FAMILY

Guide

4:10-11	Listen, my son, accept what I say, and the years of your life will be many. [11] I **guide** you in the way of wisdom and lead you along straight paths.	3723

Instruction

1:8-9	Listen, my son, to your father's **instruction** and do not forsake your mother's teaching. [9] They will be a garland to grace your head and a chain to adorn your neck.	4592
4:1-4	Listen, my sons, to a father's **instruction**; pay attention and gain understanding. [2] I give you sound learning, so do not forsake my teaching. [3] When I was a boy in my father's house, still tender, and an only child of my mother, [4] he taught me and said, "Lay hold of my words with all your heart; keep my commands and you will live."	4592
13:1	A wise son heeds his father's **instruction**, but a mocker does not listen to rebuke.	4592
19:27	Stop listening to **instruction**, my son, and you will stray from the words of knowledge.	4592

LAW

Like the 55 miles-per-hour speed limit and the seat belt law, there are spiritual rules that save lives. Proverbs does not write its principles in tablets of stone such as Exodus does. Rather it uses pithy, easy-to-remember maxims that point out for us the choices that will bring success and those that will yield disaster. This chapter emphasizes the importance of a parent who points out, based on the authoritative guidance of the Word of God, the way for his child to go.

THE LAW AND THE FAMILY		REFERENCE NUMBERS
Command		
2:1-5	My son, if you accept my words and store up my **commands** within you, [2] turning your ear to wisdom and applying your heart to understanding, [3] and if you call out for insight and cry aloud for understanding, [4] and if you look for it as for silver and search for it as for hidden treasure, [5] then you will understand the fear of the LORD and find the knowledge of God.	5184
3:1-2	My son, do not forget my teaching, but keep my **commands** in your heart, [2] for they will prolong your life many years and bring you prosperity.	5184
4:1-4	Listen, my sons, to a father's instruction; pay attention and gain understanding. [2] I give you sound learning, so do not forsake my teaching. [3] When I was a boy in my father's house, still tender, and an only child of my mother, [4] he taught me and said, "Lay hold of my words with all your heart; keep my **commands** and you will live."	5184
6:20-24	My son, keep your father's **commands** and do not forsake your mother's teaching. [21] Bind them upon your heart forever; fasten them around your neck. [22] When you walk, they will guide you; when you sleep, they will watch over you; when you awake, they will speak to you. [23] For these **commands** are a lamp, this teaching is a light, and the corrections of discipline are the way to life, [24] keeping you from the immoral woman, from the smooth tongue of the wayward wife.	5184/5184
7:1-3	My son, keep my words and store up my **commands** within you. [2] Keep my commands and you will live; guard my teachings as the apple of your eye. [3] Bind them on your fingers; write them on the tablet of your heart.	5184/5184
Instruction		
31:26	She speaks with wisdom, and faithful **instruction** is on her tongue.	9368
Law		
28:7	He who keeps the **law** is a discerning son, but a companion of gluttons disgraces his father.	9368
Teaching		
1:8	Listen, my son, to your father's instruction and do not forsake your mother's **teaching**.	9368

THE LAW AND GOD

Command		
8:27-29	I was there when he set the heavens in place, when he marked out the horizon on the face of the deep, [28] when he established the clouds above and fixed securely the fountains of the	7023

deep, [29] when he gave the sea its boundary so the waters would not overstep his **command**, and when he marked out the foundations of the earth.

Law

28:9   If anyone turns a deaf ear to the **law**, even his prayers are detestable.   9368

THE LAW AND THE WISE

Command

10:8   The wise in heart accept **commands**, but a chattering fool comes to ruin.   5184

13:13   He who scorns instruction will pay for it, but he who respects a **command** is rewarded.   5184

Instructions

19:16   He who obeys **instructions** guards his life, but he who is contemptuous of his ways will die.   5184

Law

28:4   Those who forsake the **law** praise the wicked, but those who keep the law resist them.   9368

29:18   Where there is no revelation, the people cast off restraint; but blessed is he who keeps the **law**.   9368

Teaching

13:14   The **teaching** of the wise is a fountain of life, turning a man from the snares of death.   9368

THE LAW AND CONSEQUENCES

Contemptuous

19:16   He who obeys instructions guards his life, but he who is **contemptuous** of his ways will die.   1022

Fool

10:8   The wise in heart accept commands, but a chattering **fool** comes to ruin.   211

Gluttons

28:7   He who keeps the law is a discerning son, but a companion of **gluttons** disgraces his father.   2361

Law

31:4-5   "It is not for kings, O Lemuel—not for kings to drink wine, not for rulers to crave beer, [5] lest they drink and forget what the **law** decrees, and deprive all the oppressed of their rights."   NIH

Scorns

13:13   He who **scorns** instruction will pay for it, but he who respects a command is rewarded.   996

Wicked

28:4   Those who forsake the law praise the **wicked**, but those who keep the law resist them.   8401

LAZINESS

Laziness could run a competitive race for the most underrated sin. Quietly it anesthetizes its victim into a lifeless stupor that ends in hunger, bondage, and death. The symptoms? Drowsiness, unreliability, unrealistic fantasies, excuses, pride. As one of the world's most unproductive individuals "Sam Sluggard" should get out of bed, go outside, get down on his hands and knees, and take a long, hard look at some ants. He might learn a lesson or two.

		REFERENCE NUMBERS
LAZINESS AND SLEEP		

Sleep

6:9-11	How long will you lie there, you sluggard? When will you get up from your **sleep**? [10] A little **sleep**, a little slumber, a little folding of the hands to rest—[11] and poverty will come on you like a bandit and scarcity like an armed man.	9104/9104
10:5	He who gathers crops in summer is a wise son, but he who **sleeps** during harvest is a disgraceful son.	8101
19:15	Laziness brings on deep **sleep**, and the shiftless man goes hungry.	9554
20:13	Do not love **sleep** or you will grow poor; stay awake and you will have food to spare.	9104
24:32-34	I applied my heart to what I observed and learned a lesson from what I saw: [33] A little **sleep**, a little slumber, a little folding of the hands to rest—[34] and poverty will come on you like a bandit and scarcity like an armed man.	9104

Sluggard

| 26:14 | As a door turns on its hinges, so a **sluggard** turns on his bed. | 6789 |

LAZINESS AND WISDOM

Sluggard

| 6:6-8 | Go to the ant, you **sluggard**; consider its ways and be wise! [7] It has no commander, no overseer or ruler, [8] yet it stores its provisions in summer and gathers its food at harvest. | 6789 |

LAZINESS AND UNRELIABILITY

Sluggard

| 10:26 | As vinegar to the teeth and smoke to the eyes, so is a **sluggard** to those who send him. | 6789 |

LAZINESS AND WORK

Slack

| 18:9 | One who is **slack** in his work is brother to one who destroys. | 8332 |

Sluggard

| 21:25 | The **sluggard's** craving will be the death of him, because his hands refuse to work. | 6789 |

LAZINESS AND AMBITION

Sluggard

| 13:4 | The **sluggard** craves and gets nothing, but the desires of the diligent are fully satisfied. | 6789 |
| 15:19 | The way of the **sluggard** is blocked with thorns, but the path of the upright is a highway. | 6789 |

LAZINESS AND IDLENESS

Laziness

12:24   Diligent hands will rule, but **laziness** ends in slave labor.   8244

Lazy

12:27   The **lazy** man does not roast his game, but the diligent man prizes his possessions.   8244

Sluggard

19:24   The **sluggard** buries his hand in the dish; he will not even bring it back to his mouth!   6789

24:30-31   I went past the field of the **sluggard**, past the vineyard of the man who lacks judgment; [31] thorns had come up everywhere, the ground was covered with weeds, and the stone wall was in ruins.   6789

26:15   The **sluggard** buries his hand in the dish; he is too lazy to bring it back to his mouth.   6789

LAZINESS AND EXCUSES

Sluggard

20:4   A **sluggard** does not plow in season; so at harvest time he looks but finds nothing.   6789

22:13   The **sluggard** says, "There is a lion outside!" or, "I will be murdered in the streets!"   6789

26:13   The **sluggard** says, "There is a lion in the road, a fierce lion roaming the streets!"   6789

26:16   The **sluggard** is wiser in his own eyes than seven men who answer discreetly.   6789

LIFE

Life or death results from our core beliefs. Reverence for God, respect for His instructions, and obedience to His blueprint—these constitute wisdom, and wisdom promises the gift of life. Death itself cannot extinguish the fire of life burning in the person who trusts in God with his entire heart. In Hebrew *heart* refers to more than the blood pump of the circulatory system, or the seat of our emotions. It represents our entire personality—intellect, emotion, and will—with the stress falling on the will as dynamically determining life's direction. Choices! All of us make them, and they expose our heart's condition; therefore frequent heart exams are vital. Perhaps it's time for a spiritual "treadmill" test. "Above all else, guard your heart, for it is the wellspring of life" (Prov. 4:23).

LIFE RELATED TO WISDOM AND UNDERSTANDING		REFERENCE NUMBERS
Heart		
2:1-2	My son, if you accept my words and store up my commands within you, [2] turning your ear to wisdom and applying your **heart** to understanding,	4213
10:8	The wise in **heart** accept commands, but a chattering fool comes to ruin.	4213
14:33	Wisdom reposes in the **heart** of the discerning and even among fools she lets herself be known.	4213
15:14	The discerning **heart** seeks knowledge, but the mouth of a fool feeds on folly.	4213
16:21	The wise in **heart** are called discerning, and pleasant words promote instruction.	4213
18:15	The **heart** of the discerning acquires knowledge; the ears of the wise seek it out.	4213
20:5	The purposes of a man's **heart** are deep waters, but a man of understanding draws them out.	4213
22:17	Pay attention and listen to the sayings of the wise; apply your **heart** to what I teach,	4213
Life		
3:13-18	Blessed is the man who finds wisdom, the man who gains understanding, [14] for she is more profitable than silver and yields better returns than gold. [15] She is more precious than rubies; nothing you desire can compare with her. [16] Long **life** is in her right hand; in her left hand are riches and honor. [17] Her ways are pleasant ways, and all her paths are peace. [18] She is a tree of **life** to those who embrace her; those who lay hold of her will be blessed.	3427/2644
4:13	Hold on to instruction, do not let it go; guard it well, for it is your **life**.	2644
8:35	For whoever finds me finds **life** and receives favor from the LORD.	2644
9:6	Leave your simple ways and you will **live**; walk in the way of understanding.	2649
15:24	The path of **life** leads upward for the wise to keep him from going down to the grave.	2644
15:31	He who listens to a **life-giving** rebuke will be at home among the wise.	2644

16:22 Understanding is a fountain of **life** to those who have it, but fol- 2644
ly brings punishment to fools.

Soul
24:14 Know also that wisdom is sweet to your **soul**; if you find it, 5883
there is a future hope for you, and your hope will not be cut off.

LIFE AND THE FAMILY

Heart
3:1-3 My son, do not forget my teaching, but keep my commands in 4213/4213
your **heart**, [2] for they will prolong your life many years and
bring you prosperity.
[3] Let love and faithfulness never leave you; bind them
around your neck, write them on the tablet of your **heart**.

4:4 he taught me and said, "Lay hold of my words with all your 4213
heart; keep my commands and you will live."

4:20-22 My son, pay attention to what I say; listen closely to my words. 4222
[21] Do not let them out of your sight, keep them within your
heart; [22] for they are life to those who find them and health
to a man's whole body.

6:20-23 My son, keep your father's commands and do not forsake your 4213
mother's teaching. [21] Bind them upon your **heart** forever;
fasten them around your neck. [22] When you walk, they will
guide you; when you sleep, they will watch over you; when
you awake, they will speak to you. [23] For these commands
are a lamp, this teaching is a light, and the corrections of discipline are the way to life,

7:1-3 My son, keep my words and store up my commands within 4213
you. [2] Keep my commands and you will live; guard my
teachings as the apple of your eye. [3] Bind them on your
fingers; write them on the tablet of your **heart**.

23:19 Listen, my son, and be wise, and keep your **heart** on the right 4213
path.

23:26 My son, give me your **heart** and let your eyes keep to my 4213
ways,

Life
3:21-22 My son, preserve sound judgment and discernment, do not let 2644
them out of your sight; [22] they will be **life** for you, an ornament to grace your neck.

4:10 Listen, my son, accept what I say, and the years of your **life** 2644
will be many.

31:12 She brings him good, not harm, all the days of her **life**. 2644

Soul
29:17 Discipline your son, and he will give you peace; he will bring 5883
delight to your **soul**.

LIFE AND THE LORD

Heart
1:23 If you had responded to my rebuke, I would have poured out 8120
my **heart** to you and made my thoughts known to you.

19:21 Many are the plans in a man's **heart**, but it is the Lord's pur- 4213
pose that prevails.

23:12 Apply your **heart** to instruction and your ears to words of 4213
knowledge.

		REFERENCE
LIFE AND TRUSTING GOD		NUMBERS

Heart

3:5-6   Trust in the LORD with all your **heart** and lean not on your own understanding; [6] in all your ways acknowledge him, and he will make your paths straight.   4213

15:11   Death and Destruction lie open before the LORD—how much more the **hearts** of men!   4213

16:9   In his **heart** a man plans his course, but the LORD determines his steps.   4213

17:3   The crucible for silver and the furnace for gold, but the LORD tests the **heart**.   4213

21:1-2   The king's **heart** is in the hand of the LORD; he directs it like a watercourse wherever he pleases. [2] All a man's ways seem right to him, but the LORD weighs the **heart**.   4213/4213

23:17   Do not let your **heart** envy sinners, but always be zealous for the fear of the LORD.   4213

24:12   If you say, "But we knew nothing about this," does not he who weighs the **heart** perceive it? Does not he who guards your life know it? Will he not repay each person according to what he has done?   4213

28:14   Blessed is the man who always fears the LORD, but he who hardens his **heart** falls into trouble.   4213

Life

9:10-11   "The fear of the LORD is the beginning of wisdom, and knowledge of the Holy One is understanding. [11] For through me your days will be many, and years will be added to your **life**."   2644

11:30   The fruit of the righteous is a tree of **life**, and he who wins souls is wise.   2644

14:27   The fear of the LORD is a fountain of **life**, turning a man from the snares of death.   2644

19:23   The fear of the LORD leads to **life**: Then one rests content, untouched by trouble.   2644

22:4   Humility and the fear of the LORD bring wealth and honor and **life**.   2644

Motives

16:2   All a man's ways seem innocent to him, but **motives** are weighed by the LORD.   8120

Spirit

20:27   The lamp of the LORD searches the **spirit** of a man; it searches out his inmost being.   5972

LIFE AND DISCIPLINE

Heart

4:23   Above all else, guard your **heart**, for it is the wellspring of life.   4213

5:12   You will say, "How I hated discipline! How my **heart** spurned correction!"   4213

10:8   The wise in **heart** accept commands, but a chattering fool comes to ruin.   4213

22:15   Folly is bound up in the **heart** of a child, but the rod of discipline will drive it far from him.   4213

24:17   Do not gloat when your enemy falls; when he stumbles, do not let your **heart** rejoice,   4213

Life

10:16-17 The wages of the righteous bring them **life**, but the income of   2644/2644
the wicked brings them punishment. [17] He who heeds disci-
pline shows the way to **life**, but whoever ignores correction
leads others astray.

15:31   He who listens to a **life-giving** rebuke will be at home among   2644
the wise.

Soul

22:5   In the paths of the wicked lie thorns and snares, but he who   5883
guards his **soul** stays far from them.

23:13-14 Do not withhold discipline from a child; if you punish him with   5883
the rod, he will not die. [14] Punish him with the rod and save
his **soul** from death.

29:17   Discipline your son, and he will give you peace; he will bring   5883
delight to your **soul**.

LIFE AND ENCOURAGEMENT

Heart

12:25   An anxious **heart** weighs a man down, but a kind word cheers   4213
him up.

13:12   Hope deferred makes the **heart** sick, but a longing fulfilled is a   4213
tree of life.

15:13   A happy **heart** makes the face cheerful, but heartache crushes   4213
the spirit.

15:15   All the days of the oppressed are wretched, but the cheerful   4213
heart has a continual feast.

15:30   A cheerful look brings joy to the **heart**, and good news gives   4213
health to the bones.

17:22   A cheerful **heart** is good medicine, but a crushed spirit dries up   4213
the bones.

27:9   Perfume and incense bring joy to the **heart**, and the pleasant-   4213
ness of one's friend springs from his earnest counsel.

27:19   As water reflects a face, so a man's **heart** reflects the man.   4213

Soul

16:24   Pleasant words are a honeycomb, sweet to the **soul** and healing   5883
to the bones.

25:25   Like cold water to a weary **soul** is good news from a distant   5883
land.

Spirit

25:13   Like the coolness of snow at harvest time is a trustworthy mes-   5883
senger to those who send him; he refreshes the **spirit** of his
masters.

LIFE AND DISCOURAGEMENT

Anguish

31:6   Give beer to those who are perishing, wine to those who are in   5253 + 5883
anguish;

Heart

14:10   Each **heart** knows its own bitterness, and no one else can share   4213
its joy.

25:20   Like one who takes away a garment on a cold day, or like vine-   4213
gar poured on soda, is one who sings songs to a heavy **heart**.

Spirit

18:14   A man's **spirit** sustains him in sickness, but a crushed **spirit**   8120/8120
who can bear?

LIFE AND THE TONGUE

Calamity

21:23   He who guards his mouth and his tongue keeps himself from   7650
calamity.

Heart

10:20   The tongue of the righteous is choice silver, but the **heart** of   4213
the wicked is of little value.

15:7   The lips of the wise spread knowledge; not so the **hearts** of   4213
fools.

15:28   The **heart** of the righteous weighs its answers, but the mouth of   4213
the wicked gushes evil.

16:23   A wise man's **heart** guides his mouth, and his lips promote in-   4213
struction.

22:11   He who loves a pure **heart** and whose speech is gracious will   4213
have the king for his friend.

Life

10:11   The mouth of the righteous is a fountain of **life**, but violence   2644
overwhelms the mouth of the wicked.

13:3   He who guards his lips guards his **life**, but he who speaks rash-   5883
ly will come to ruin.

15:4   The tongue that brings healing is a tree of **life**, but a deceitful   2644
tongue crushes the spirit.

18:21   The tongue has the power of **life** and death, and those who love   2644
it will eat its fruit.

Soul

16:24   Pleasant words are a honeycomb, sweet to the **soul** and healing   5883
to the bones.

LIFE AND IMMORALITY

Destroys

6:32   But a man who commits adultery lacks judgment; whoever   8845
does so **destroys** himself.

Life

5:6   She gives no thought to the way of **life**; her paths are crooked,   2644
but she knows it not.

6:26   for the prostitute reduces you to a loaf of bread, and the adulter-   5883
ess preys upon your very **life**.

7:22-23   All at once he followed her like an ox going to the slaughter,   5883
like a deer stepping into a noose [23] till an arrow pierces his
liver, like a bird darting into a snare, little knowing it will cost
him his **life**.

LIFE AND THE WICKED

Heart

6:12-15   A scoundrel and villain, who goes about with a corrupt mouth,   4213
[13] who winks with his eye, signals with his feet and motions
with his fingers, [14] who plots evil with deceit in his **heart**—
he always stirs up dissension. [15] Therefore disaster will overtake him in an instant; he will suddenly be destroyed—without
remedy.

6:16-19	There are six things the Lord hates, seven that are detestable to him: [17] haughty eyes, a lying tongue, hands that shed innocent blood, [18] a **heart** that devises wicked schemes, feet that are quick to rush into evil, [19] a false witness who pours out lies and a man who stirs up dissension among brothers.	4213
10:20	The tongue of the righteous is choice silver, but the **heart** of the wicked is of little value.	4213
11:20	The Lord detests men of perverse **heart** but he delights in those whose ways are blameless.	4213
12:20	There is deceit in the **hearts** of those who plot evil, but joy for those who promote peace.	4213
17:20	A man of perverse **heart** does not prosper; he whose tongue is deceitful falls into trouble.	4213
23:7	for he is the kind of man who is always thinking about the cost. "Eat and drink," he says to you, but his **heart** is not with you.	4213
24:2	for their **hearts** plot violence, and their lips talk about making trouble.	4213
26:23-25	Like a coating of glaze over earthenware are fervent lips with an evil **heart**. [24] A malicious man disguises himself with his lips, but in his **heart** he harbors deceit. [25] Though his speech is charming, do not believe him, for seven abominations fill his **heart**.	4213/7931/ 4213

Life

1:18-19	These men lie in wait for their own blood; they waylay only themselves! [19] Such is the end of all who go after ill-gotten gain; it takes away the **lives** of those who get it.	5883

LIFE AND THE RIGHTEOUS

Heart

15:28	The **heart** of the righteous weighs its answers, but the mouth of the wicked gushes evil.	4213

Life

10:16	The wages of the righteous bring them **life**, but the income of the wicked brings them punishment.	2644
11:19	The truly righteous man attains **life**, but he who pursues evil goes to his death.	2644
11:30	The fruit of the righteous is a tree of **life**, and he who wins souls is wise.	2644
12:28	In the way of righteousness there is **life**; along that path is immortality.	2644
16:17	The highway of the upright avoids evil; he who guards his way guards his **life**.	5883
21:21	He who pursues righteousness and love finds **life**, prosperity and honor.	2644

LIFE AND THE FOOL

Heart

12:23	A prudent man keeps his knowledge to himself, but the **heart** of fools blurts out folly.	4213
15:7	The lips of the wise spread knowledge; not so the **hearts** of fools.	4213
19:3	A man's own folly ruins his life, yet his **heart** rages against the Lord.	4213

Soul

18:7   A fool's mouth is his undoing, and his lips are a snare to his   5883
soul.

LOVE

In Proverbs "love" begins with the conscious choice of God's wisdom and His righteousness, and the deliberate rejection of foolishness and sin. It is God's mysterious gift that expresses itself in kindness to the needy, care in the use of language, and intoxicating sexual pleasure enjoyed by a husband and wife. Love tenderly cloaks in silence what is displeasing in another, but strongly applies the rod of correction when discipline demands it. Love forgives and covers sin. Love is kind feeling and action for others. Love for sinners moved God to give His Son. "This is love: not that we loved God, but that he loved us and sent his Son as an atoning sacrifice for our sins" (1 John 4:10).

		REFERENCE NUMBERS
LOVE AND HAPPINESS		
Bless		
14:21	He who despises his neighbor sins, but **blessed** is he who is kind to the needy.	897
Love		
14:22	Do not those who plot evil go astray? But those who plan what is good find **love** and faithfulness.	2876
LOVE AND THE FEAR OF THE LORD		
Love		
3:3	Let **love** and faithfulness never leave you; bind them around your neck, write them on the tablet of your heart.	2876
15:9	The LORD detests the way of the wicked but he **loves** those who pursue righteousness.	170
16:6	Through **love** and faithfulness sin is atoned for; through the fear of the LORD a man avoids evil.	2876
21:21	He who pursues righteousness and **love** finds life, prosperity and honor.	2876
LOVE AND HOPE		
Hope		
19:18	Discipline your son, for in that there is **hope**; do not be a willing party to his death.	9536
Kind		
12:25	An anxious heart weighs a man down, but a **kind** word cheers him up.	3202
Longing		
13:12	Hope deferred makes the heart sick, but a **longing** fulfilled is a tree of life.	9294
LOVE AND THE TONGUE		
Joy		
15:23	A man finds **joy** in giving an apt reply—and how good is a timely word!	8525
Love		
18:21	The tongue has the power of life and death, and those who **love** it will eat its fruit.	170
LOVE RELATED TO FRIENDS AND ENEMIES		
Gloat		
17:5	He who mocks the poor shows contempt for their Maker; whoever **gloats** over disaster will not go unpunished.	8523

		REFERENCE NUMBERS
24:17	Do not **gloat** when your enemy falls; when he stumbles, do not let your heart rejoice,	8523

Love

| 17:17 | A friend **loves** at all times, and a brother is born for adversity. | 170 |

LOVE AND THE FAMILY

Love

5:19	A loving doe, a graceful deer—may her breasts satisfy you always, may you ever be captivated by her **love**.	173
13:24	He who spares the rod hates his son, but he who **loves** him is careful to discipline him.	170
29:3	A man who **loves** wisdom brings joy to his father, but a companion of prostitutes squanders his wealth.	170

Rejoice

| 5:18 | May your fountain be blessed, and may you **rejoice** in the wife of your youth. | 8523 |

LOVE AND WISDOM

Love

4:6	Do not forsake wisdom, and she will protect you; **love** her, and she will watch over you.	170
8:17-21	I **love** those who **love** me, and those who seek me find me. [18] With me are riches and honor, enduring wealth and prosperity. [19] My fruit is better than fine gold; what I yield surpasses choice silver. [20] I walk in the way of righteousness, along the paths of justice, [21] bestowing wealth on those who **love** me and making their treasuries full.	170/170/170
19:8	He who gets wisdom **loves** his own soul; he who cherishes understanding prospers.	170

LOVE AND FORGIVENESS

Love

10:12	Hatred stirs up dissension, but **love** covers over all wrongs.	173
15:17	Better a meal of vegetables where there is **love** than a fattened calf with hatred.	173
17:9	He who covers over an offense promotes **love**, but whoever repeats the matter separates close friends.	173

Mercy

| 28:13 | He who conceals his sins does not prosper, but whoever confesses and renounces them finds **mercy**. | 8163 |

LOVE AND HONEST CONFRONTATION

Love

| 9:8 | Do not rebuke a mocker or he will hate you; rebuke a wise man and he will **love** you. | 170 |
| 27:5 | Better is open rebuke than hidden **love**. | 173 |

LOVE AND DEATH

Love

| 8:36 | "But whoever fails to find me harms himself; all who hate me **love** death." | 170 |

LYING

Like cruel violence, lying is a fundamental characteristic of evil. One of the "Abominable Seven"—things God detests—lies turn lawsuits into vicious miscarriages of justice and governments into violent anarchies. From the charm of a seductive woman to the syrupy flattery of the business con, deceit masks the greed and hatred of a wicked, malicious heart. Lies can generate wealth, power, and success, but neither liars nor their wealth can stand the test of time. Ironically, liars slowly believe their own falsehoods, but in the ultimate divine courtroom all lies will be exposed and judged.

LYING AND DECEIT		REFERENCE NUMBERS
Deceit		
12:5	The plans of the righteous are just, but the advice of the wicked is **deceitful**.	5327
12:20	There is **deceit** in the hearts of those who plot evil, but joy for those who promote peace.	5327
14:8	The wisdom of the prudent is to give thought to their ways, but the folly of fools is **deception**.	5327
24:28	Do not testify against your neighbor without cause, or use your lips to **deceive**.	7331
26:19	is a man who **deceives** his neighbor and says, "I was only joking!"	8228
31:30	Charm is **deceptive**, and beauty is fleeting; but a woman who fears the Lord is to be praised.	9214
Fraud		
20:17	Food gained by **fraud** tastes sweet to a man, but he ends up with a mouth full of gravel.	9214
Lying		
21:6	A fortune made by a **lying** tongue is a fleeting vapor and a deadly snare.	9214

LYING AND HATRED		
Deceit		
26:24-26	A malicious man disguises himself with his lips, but in his heart he harbors **deceit**. [25] Though his speech is charming, do not believe him, for seven abominations fill his heart. [26] His malice may be concealed by deception, but his wickedness will be exposed in the assembly.	5327
Lying		
10:18	He who conceals his hatred has **lying** lips, and whoever spreads slander is a fool.	9214
26:28	A **lying** tongue hates those it hurts, and a flattering mouth works ruin.	9214

LYING AND A FALSE WITNESS		
Deceit		
14:25	A truthful witness saves lives, but a false witness is **deceitful**.	5327
Liar		
30:6	Do not add to his words, or he will rebuke you and prove you a **liar**.	3941

REFERENCE
NUMBERS

Lies

12:17   A truthful witness gives honest testimony, but a false witness   5327
tells **lies**.

14:5   A truthful witness does not deceive, but a false witness pours   3942
out **lies**.

19:5   A false witness will not go unpunished, and he who pours out   3942
lies will not go free.

19:9   A false witness will not go unpunished, and he who pours out   3942
lies will perish.

LYING AND THE TONGUE

Liar

17:4   A wicked man listens to evil lips; a **liar** pays attention to a ma-   9214
licious tongue.

Lies

6:16-19   There are six things the LORD hates, seven that are detestable to   3942
him: [17] haughty eyes, a lying tongue, hands that shed inno-
cent blood, [18] a heart that devises wicked schemes, feet that
are quick to rush into evil, [19] a false witness who pours out
lies and a man who stirs up dissension among brothers.

Lying

12:19   Truthful lips endure forever, but a **lying** tongue lasts only a mo-   9214
ment.

12:22   The LORD detests **lying** lips, but he delights in men who are   9214
truthful.

LYING AND AUTHORITIES

Lies

29:12   If a ruler listens to **lies**, all his officials become wicked.   1821 + 9214

Lying

17:7   Arrogant lips are unsuited to a fool—how much worse **lying**   9214
lips to a ruler!

CONTRASTS TO LYING

Falsehood/Lies

30:7-9   "Two things I ask of you, O LORD; do not refuse me before I   8736/
die: [8] Keep **falsehood** and **lies** far from me; give me neither   1821 + 3942
poverty nor riches, but give me only my daily bread. [9] Other-
wise, I may have too much and disown you and say, 'Who is
the LORD?' Or I may become poor and steal, and so dishonor
the name of my God."

Plans

12:5   The **plans** of the righteous are just, but the advice of the wicked   4742
is deceitful.

Prudent

14:8   The wisdom of the **prudent** is to give thought to their ways,   6874
but the folly of fools is deception.

Righteous

13:5   The **righteous** hate what is false, but the wicked bring shame   7404
and disgrace.

Truthful

12:17   A **truthful** witness gives honest testimony, but a false witness   575
tells lies.

		REFERENCE NUMBERS
12:19	**Truthful** lips endure forever, but a lying tongue lasts only a moment.	622
12:22	The LORD detests lying lips, but he delights in men who are **truthful**.	575
14:5	A **truthful** witness does not deceive, but a false witness pours out lies.	574
14:25	A **truthful** witness saves lives, but a false witness is deceitful.	622

MORALITY

Morality is the science and art of learning to make right decisions. The fool's "thoughtlessness" concerning ethical values trashes his life. The wise individual's "thoughtfulness" yields security and protection. Wisdom believes God's standards recorded in Scripture, and learns what they mean and how to apply them in real life situations. Wisdom believes that patience, discretion, self-control, prudence, and purity still apply in the 1990s. "Our fathers disciplined us for a little while as they thought best; but God disciplines us for our good, that we may share in his holiness" (Heb. 12:10).

		REFERENCE NUMBERS
MORALITY AND SELF-CONTROL		

Patience

| 19:11 | A man's wisdom gives him **patience**; it is to his glory to overlook an offense. | 678 + 799 |

MORALITY AND SOUND JUDGMENT

Discerning

| 16:21 | The wise in heart are called **discerning**, and pleasant words promote instruction. | 1067 |
| 18:15 | The heart of the **discerning** acquires knowledge; the ears of the wise seek it out. | 1067 |

Discernment

| 3:21-22 | My son, preserve sound judgment and **discernment**, do not let them out of your sight; [22] they will be life for you, an ornament to grace your neck. | 4659 |

Discretion

1:4	for giving prudence to the simple, knowledge and **discretion** to the young—	4659
2:10-11	For wisdom will enter your heart, and knowledge will be pleasant to your soul. [11] **Discretion** will protect you, and understanding will guard you.	4659
5:1-2	My son, pay attention to my wisdom, listen well to my words of insight, [2] that you may maintain **discretion** and your lips may preserve knowledge.	4659

Prudent

12:16	A fool shows his annoyance at once, but a **prudent** man overlooks an insult.	6874
12:23	A **prudent** man keeps his knowledge to himself, but the heart of fools blurts out folly.	6874
13:16	Every **prudent** man acts out of knowledge, but a fool exposes his folly.	6874
14:8	The wisdom of the **prudent** is to give thought to their ways, but the folly of fools is deception.	6874
14:15	A simple man believes anything, but a **prudent** man gives thought to his steps.	6874
14:18	The simple inherit folly, but the **prudent** are crowned with knowledge.	6874
22:3	A **prudent** man sees danger and takes refuge, but the simple keep going and suffer for it.	6874
27:12	The **prudent** see danger and take refuge, but the simple keep going and suffer for it.	6874

MORALITY AND VIRTUE		REFERENCE NUMBERS

Innocent

21:8 The way of the guilty is devious, but the conduct of the **innocent** is upright.   3838

Noble

12:4 A wife of **noble** character is her husband's crown, but a disgraceful wife is like decay in his bones.   2657

31:10 A wife of **noble** character who can find? She is worth far more than rubies.   2657

31:29 "Many women do **noble** things, but you surpass them all."   2657

Prudent

8:12 "I, wisdom, dwell together with **prudence**; I possess knowledge and discretion."   6893

19:14 Houses and wealth are inherited from parents, but a **prudent** wife is from the LORD.   8505

Pure

20:9 Who can say, "I have kept my heart **pure**; I am clean and without sin"?   2342

20:11 Even a child is known by his actions, by whether his conduct is **pure** and right.   2341

MORALITY RELATED TO THOUGHT AND SPEECH

Pure

15:26 The LORD detests the thoughts of the wicked, but those of the **pure** are pleasing to him.   3196

22:11 He who loves a **pure** heart and whose speech is gracious will have the king for his friend.   3196

NATURE

In Proverbs nature is an artistic masterpiece, the handwork of the divine genius. According to chapter 8, God's blueprint guided the divine construction project; thus the careful observation of nature can help us to learn to live. From the refreshing sound of a bubbling brook to the despair of rainless clouds, the wise individual sees penetrating object lessons in nature revealing life experience. Romans 1 speaks of two sources of divine revelation—the Holy Scripture and nature. The inspiration of Proverbs teaches us how to read God's thoughts in nature.

NATURE AND THE LORD

		REFERENCE NUMBERS
Clouds		
3:19-20	By wisdom the LORD laid the earth's foundations, by understanding he set the heavens in place; [20] by his knowledge the deeps were divided, and the **clouds** let drop the dew.	8836
8:27-31	I was there when he set the heavens in place, when he marked out the horizon on the face of the deep, [28] when he established the **clouds** above and fixed securely the fountains of the deep, [29] when he gave the sea its boundary so the waters would not overstep his command, and when he marked out the foundations of the earth. [30] Then I was the craftsman at his side. I was filled with delight day after day, rejoicing always in his presence, [31] rejoicing in his whole world and delighting in mankind.	8836
Earth		
30:4	Who has gone up to heaven and come down? Who has gathered up the wind in the hollow of his hands? Who has wrapped up the waters in his cloak? Who has established all the ends of the **earth**? What is his name, and the name of his son? Tell me if you know!	824
Oceans		
8:24-26	When there were no **oceans**, I was given birth, when there were no springs abounding with water; [25] before the mountains were settled in place, before the hills, I was given birth, [26] before he made the earth or its fields or any of the dust of the world.	9333

NATURE AND AUTHORITIES

Heavens		
25:3	As the **heavens** are high and the earth is deep, so the hearts of kings are unsearchable.	9028
Rain		
16:15	When a king's face brightens, it means life; his favor is like a **rain** cloud in spring.	4919
Snow		
25:13	Like the coolness of **snow** at harvest time is a trustworthy messenger to those who send him; he refreshes the spirit of his masters.	8920
Watercourse		
21:1	The king's heart is in the hand of the LORD; he directs it like a **watercourse** wherever he pleases.	4784 + 7104

NATURE RELATED TO THE FOOL AND THE TONGUE

THE FOOL

Snow		
26:1	Like **snow** in summer or rain in harvest, honor is not fitting for a fool.	8920

THE TONGUE

Rain

25:23   As a north wind brings **rain**, so a sly tongue brings angry   4784
looks.

Waters

18:4   The words of a man's mouth are deep **waters**, but the fountain   4784
of wisdom is a bubbling brook.

NATURE AND COUNSEL

Waters

20:5   The purposes of a man's heart are deep **waters**, but a man of   4784
understanding draws them out.

27:19   As **water** reflects a face, so a man's heart reflects the man.   4784

NATURE RELATED TO PRIDE AND STRIFE

PRIDE

Clouds

25:14   Like **clouds** and wind without rain is a man who boasts of gifts   5955
he does not give.

STRIFE

Rainy

27:15   A quarrelsome wife is like a constant dripping on a **rainy** day;   6039

NATURE AND DILIGENCE

Summer

6:6-8   Go to the ant, you sluggard; consider its ways and be wise! [7]   7811
It has no commander, no overseer or ruler, [8] yet it stores its
provisions in **summer** and gathers its food at harvest.

10:5   He who gathers crops in **summer** is a wise son, but he who   7811
sleeps during harvest is a disgraceful son.

30:24-25   "Four things on earth are small, yet they are extremely wise: 7811
[25] Ants are creatures of little strength, yet they store up their
food in the **summer**;"

NATURE AND THE POOR

Rain

28:3   A ruler who oppresses the poor is like a driving **rain** that leaves   4764
no crops.

NUTRITION

The tragic death of an adolescent victim of anorexia and the heart failure of an obese fifty-year-old confront us with food as a major problem in our society. God's child needs to discern that food becomes devilish when idolized—"Man does not live by 'bread' alone." Sex, self, and food make poor substitutes for God. Self control at the table is an objective evidence of Spirit control in the heart. God's wisdom helps us realize that a succulent roast beef dinner in an exquisite restaurant could be just a bribe, but it also moves us to bow our heads in thanksgiving over a table filled with provisions when our Father in heaven graciously gives far more than our daily bread. Reverence and hard work, not laziness, puts food on the table, yet those with plenty dare not eat if wages are unjust, or if those too weak to labor have nothing.

		REFERENCE NUMBERS
NUTRITION AND AUTHORITIES		
Eat		
27:18	He who tends a fig tree will **eat** its fruit, and he who looks after his master will be honored.	430
Gluttony		
23:1-3	When you sit to dine with a ruler, note well what is before you, [2] and put a knife to your throat if you are given to **gluttony**. [3] Do not crave his delicacies, for that food is deceptive.	1251 + 5883

NUTRITION AND IMMORALITY

Bread		
6:26	for the prostitute reduces you to a loaf of **bread**, and the adulteress preys upon your very life.	4312
Eat		
9:17	"Stolen water is sweet; food **eaten** in secret is delicious!"	NIH
30:20	"This is the way of an adulteress: She **eats** and wipes her mouth and says, 'I've done nothing wrong.'"	430
Honey		
5:3	For the lips of an adulteress drip **honey**, and her speech is smoother than oil;	5885

NUTRITION AND THE RIGHTEOUS

Eat		
13:25	The righteous **eat** to their hearts' content, but the stomach of the wicked goes hungry.	430
Nourish		
10:21	The lips of the righteous **nourish** many, but fools die for lack of judgment.	8286

NUTRITION RELATED TO DECEIT AND PRIDE

DECEIT

Food		
20:17	**Food** gained by fraud tastes sweet to a man, but he ends up with a mouth full of gravel.	4312
23:6-8	Do not eat the **food** of a stingy man, do not crave his delicacies; [7] for he is the kind of man who is always thinking about the cost. "Eat and drink," he says to you, but his heart is not with you. [8] You will vomit up the little you have eaten and will have wasted your compliments.	4312

PRIDE

Food

12:9   Better to be a nobody and yet have a servant than pretend to be   4312
somebody and have no **food**.

Honey

25:27   It is not good to eat too much **honey**, nor is it honorable to seek   1831
one's own honor.

NUTRITION AND WORK

Food

6:6-8   Go to the ant, you sluggard; consider its ways and be wise! [7]   4407
It has no commander, no overseer or ruler, [8] yet it stores its
provisions in summer and gathers its **food** at harvest.

12:11   He who works his land will have abundant **food**, but he who   4312
chases fantasies lacks judgment.

20:13   Do not love sleep or you will grow poor; stay awake and you   4312
will have **food** to spare.

28:19   He who works his land will have abundant **food**, but the one   4312
who chases fantasies will have his fill of poverty.

30:25   Ants are creatures of little strength, yet they store up their **food**   4312
in the summer;

Hunger

16:26   The laborer's appetite works for him; his **hunger** drives him   7023
on.

NUTRITION AND GIVING

Food

22:9   A generous man will himself be blessed, for he shares his **food**   4312
with the poor.

25:21   If your enemy is hungry, give him **food** to eat; if he is thirsty,   4312
give him water to drink.

Generous

11:25   A **generous** man will prosper; he who refreshes others will   1388
himself be refreshed.

NUTRITION AND THE VIRTUOUS WIFE

Bread

31:27   She watches over the affairs of her household and does not eat   4312
the **bread** of idleness.

Food

31:14-15 She is like the merchant ships, bringing her **food** from afar.   4312/3272
[15] She gets up while it is still dark; she provides **food** for her
family and portions for her servant girls.

NUTRITION AND THE TONGUE

Eat

18:21   The tongue has the power of life and death, and those who love   430
it will **eat** its fruit.

Fruit

13:2   From the **fruit** of his lips a man enjoys good things, but the un-   7262
faithful have a craving for violence.

Honey

16:24   Pleasant words are a **honeycomb**, sweet to the soul and healing   1831 + 7430
to the bones.

27:7   He who is full loathes **honey**, but to the hungry even what is   5885
bitter tastes sweet.

NUTRITION RELATED TO DISOBEDIENCE AND THE WICKED

DISOBEDIENCE

Eaten

30:17   "The eye that mocks a father, that scorns obedience to a moth-   430
er, will be pecked out by the ravens of the valley, will be **eaten**
by the vultures."

THE WICKED

Meat

23:20-21 Do not join those who drink too much wine or gorge them-   1414
selves on **meat**, [21] for drunkards and gluttons become poor,
and drowsiness clothes them in rags.

NUTRITION RELATED TO CONTENTMENT AND HEALTH

CONTENTMENT

Bread

30:8   Keep falsehood and lies far from me; give me neither poverty   2976 + 4312
nor riches, but give me only my daily **bread**.

HEALTH

Feast

15:15   All the days of the oppressed are wretched, but the cheerful   5492
heart has a continual **feast**.

Health

3:7-8   Do not be wise in your own eyes; fear the LORD and shun evil.   8326
[8] This will bring **health** to your body and nourishment to
your bones.

15:30   A cheerful look brings joy to the heart, and good news gives   2014
health to the bones.

Honey

24:13   Eat **honey**, my son, for it is good; **honey** from the comb is   1831/5885
sweet to your taste.

25:16   If you find **honey**, eat just enough—too much of it, and you   1831
will vomit.

Nourish

27:27   You will have plenty of goats' milk to feed you and your family   2644
and to **nourish** your servant girls.

NUTRITION AND THE FOOL

Feeds

15:14   The discerning heart seeks knowledge, but the mouth of a fool   8286
feeds on folly.

Food

30:20-23 "This is the way of an adulteress: She eats and wipes her   4312
mouth and says, 'I've done nothing wrong.'
[21] "Under three things the earth trembles, under four it
cannot bear up: [22] a servant who becomes king, a fool who is
full of **food,** [23] an unloved woman who is married, and a
maidservant who displaces her mistress."

NUTRITION AND HUNGER

Food

12:9   Better to be a nobody and yet have a servant than pretend to be somebody and have no **food**.   4312

Hunger

6:30   Men do not despise a thief if he steals to satisfy his **hunger** when he is starving.   5883

Hungry

13:25   The righteous eat to their hearts' content, but the stomach of the wicked goes **hungry**.   2893

19:15   Laziness brings on deep sleep, and the shiftless man goes **hungry**.   8279

THE POOR

In Proverbs we do not find the proud, simplistic conclusion that poverty is laziness, a refusal to work; nor do we find the patronizing wealthy seeking to appease their guilt by doling out welfare to the lower classes. Instead, like the prophet, the wise teacher warns government and business against the exploitation of the poor by exorbitant taxes and interest or unfair wages. Rulers who abuse the lower classes ruin a nation's productivity. White collar workers who demean the blue collar ones will find their roles reversed in time.

Proverbs captures the gloom of poverty—helplessness in court, shunned by friends and family, futile pleading before harsh bosses—but it refuses to coddle the poor or foster dependency. The wise teacher reminds them that character—honesty, dependability, discernment, godliness, and satisfaction—cannot be purchased. Abuse from the wealthy does not justify laziness in the poor. God is no respecter of persons. The Judge will set things right someday. But for now, the poor may receive free of charge what really counts for eternity.

THE POOR AND OPPRESSION		REFERENCE NUMBERS

Helpless

28:15	Like a roaring lion or a charging bear is a wicked man ruling over a **helpless** people.	1924

Needy

30:11-14	"There are those who curse their fathers and do not bless their mothers; [12] those who are pure in their own eyes and yet are not cleansed of their filth; [13] those whose eyes are ever so haughty, whose glances are so disdainful; [14] those whose teeth are swords and whose jaws are set with knives to devour the poor from the earth, the **needy** from among mankind."	36

Poor

13:23	A **poor** man's field may produce abundant food, but injustice sweeps it away.	8133
14:31	He who oppresses the **poor** shows contempt for their Maker, but whoever is kind to the needy honors God.	1924
17:5	He who mocks the **poor** shows contempt for their Maker; whoever gloats over disaster will not go unpunished.	8133
22:16	He who oppresses the **poor** to increase his wealth and he who gives gifts to the rich—both come to poverty.	1924
22:22	Do not exploit the **poor** because they are **poor** and do not crush the needy in court,	1924/1924
28:3	A ruler who oppresses the **poor** is like a driving rain that leaves no crops.	1924
31:9	"Speak up and judge fairly; defend the rights of the **poor** and needy."	6714

THE POOR AND GENEROSITY

Gives

11:24	One man **gives** freely, yet gains even more; another withholds unduly, but comes to poverty.	7061

Needy

14:21	He who despises his neighbor sis, but blessed is he who is kind to the **needy**.	6705

		REFERENCE NUMBERS
31:20	She opens her arms to the poor and extends her hands to the needy.	36

Poor

19:17	He who is kind to the **poor** lends to the LORD, and he will reward him for what he has done.	1924
21:13	If a man shuts his ears to the cry of the **poor**, he too will cry out and not be answered.	1924
22:9	A generous man will himself be blessed, for he shares his food with the **poor**.	1924
28:8	He who increases his wealth by exorbitant interest amasses it for another, who will be kind to the **poor**.	1924
28:27	He who gives to the **poor** will lack nothing, but he who closes his eyes to them receives many curses.	8133
29:7	The righteous care about justice for the **poor**, but the wicked have no such concern.	1924
29:14	If a king judges the **poor** with fairness, his throne will always be secure.	1924

THE POOR AND WORK

Poor

10:4	Lazy hands make a man poor, but diligent hands bring wealth.	8133
13:23	A **poor** man's field may produce abundant food, but injustice sweeps it away.	8133
30:7-9	"Two things I ask of you, O LORD; do not refuse me before I die: [8] Keep falsehood and lies far from me; give me neither poverty nor riches, but give me only my daily bread. [9] Otherwise, I may have too much and disown you and say, 'Who is the LORD?' Or I may become **poor** and steal, and so dishonor the name of my God."	3769

THE POOR AND INFLUENCE

Poor

10:15	The wealth of the rich is their fortified city, but poverty is the ruin of the **poor**.	1924
13:8	A man's riches may ransom his life, but a **poor** man hears no threat.	8133
14:20	The **poor** are shunned even by their neighbors, but the rich have many friends.	8133
18:23	A **poor** man pleads for mercy, but a rich man answers harshly.	8133
19:1	Better a **poor** man whose walk is blameless than a fool whose lips are perverse.	8133
19:4	Wealth brings many friends, but a **poor** man's friend deserts him.	1924
19:7	A **poor** man is shunned by all his relatives—how much more do his friends avoid him! Though he pursues them with pleading, they are nowhere to be found.	8133
19:22	What a man desires is unfailing **love**; better to be poor than a liar.	8133

THE POOR AND THE RICH

Poor

22:2	Rich and **poor** have this in common: The LORD is the Maker of them all.	8133

REFERENCE
NUMBERS

22:7	The rich rule over the **poor**, and the borrower is servant to the lender.	8133
28:11	A rich man may be wise in his own eyes, but a **poor** man who has discernment sees through him.	1924

THE POOR AND DISCIPLINE

Poor

20:13	Do not love sleep or you will grow **poor**; stay awake and you will have food to spare.	3769
21:17	He who loves pleasure will become **poor**; whoever loves wine and oil will never be rich.	4728
23:19-21	Listen, my son, and be wise, and keep your heart on the right path. [20] Do not join those who drink too much wine or gorge themselves on meat, [21] for drunkards and gluttons become **poor**, and drowsiness clothes them in rags.	3769
28:6	Better a **poor** man whose walk is blameless than a rich man whose ways are perverse.	8133

Poverty

13:18	He who ignores discipline comes to **poverty** and shame, but whoever heeds correction is honored.	8203
28:22	A stingy man is eager to get rich and is unaware that **poverty** awaits him.	2895

PRIDE

Pride heads the list of God's "Abominable Seven." He is the mortal enemy of the proud. Proud persons act strong and tough, but the truth is they are weak and insecure. Their hard veneer in relationships causes constant hurt and quarrels. How could anyone who cannot even exist without oxygen for a few minutes believe he is indestructible? Even though every second of life is God's gracious gift, but human arrogance clinches its fist against God. Man's arrogance generated sin and death in the Garden of Eden. And God still condemns pride.

PRIDE AND BOASTING		REFERENCE NUMBERS
Boast		
20:14	"It's no good, it's no good!" says the buyer; then off he goes and **boasts** about his purchase.	2146
25:14	Like clouds and wind without rain is a man who **boasts** of gifts he does not give.	2146
27:1	Do not **boast** about tomorrow, for you do not know what a day may bring forth.	2146
Proud		
21:4	Haughty eyes and a **proud** heart, the lamp of the wicked, are sin!	8146

PRIDE AND DESTRUCTION

Pride		
15:25	The LORD tears down the **proud** man's house but he keeps the widow's boundaries intact.	1450
16:5	The LORD detests all the **proud** of heart. Be sure of this: They will not go unpunished.	1468
16:18	**Pride** goes before destruction, a haughty spirit before a fall.	1454
18:12	Before his downfall a man's heart is **proud**, but humility comes before honor.	1467
29:23	A man's **pride** brings him low, but a man of lowly spirit gains honor.	1452

PRIDE AND SHAME

Pride		
11:2	When **pride** comes, then comes disgrace, but with humility comes wisdom.	2295

PRIDE AND CONTENTIONS

Greedy		
28:25	A **greedy** man stirs up dissension, but he who trusts in the LORD will prosper.	5883 + 8146
Haughty		
6:16-19	There are six things the LORD hates, seven that are detestable to him: [17] **haughty** eyes, a lying tongue, hands that shed innocent blood, [18] a heart that devises wicked schemes, feet that are quick to rush into evil, [19] a false witness who pours out lies and a man who stirs up dissension among brothers.	8123
Pride		
13:10	**Pride** only breeds quarrels, but wisdom is found in those who take advice.	2295

21:24	The proud and arrogant man—"Mocker" is his name; he behaves with overweening **pride**.	2294

CONTRASTS TO PRIDE

Humility
11:2	When pride comes, then comes disgrace, but with **humility** comes wisdom.	7560
18:12	Before his downfall a man's heart is proud, but **humility** comes before honor.	6708

Lowly
29:23	A man's pride brings him low, but a man of **lowly** spirit gains honor.	9166

Pride
8:13	To fear the LORD is to hate evil; I hate **pride** and arrogance, evil behavior and perverse speech.	1449

Trusts
28:25	A greedy man stirs up dissension, but he who **trusts** in the LORD will prosper.	1053

Wisdom
13:10	Pride only breeds quarrels, but **wisdom** is found in those who take advice.	2683

THE RICH

The sales pitch of some television evangelists would lead us to conclude that a donation to their organization, which they identify as giving to God, is like playing a great cosmic slot machine—put a few dollars in and you will hit the jackpot. Does Scripture guarantee prosperity to those who give? Proverbs does insist that God must be honored with our money, for He is the giver of wealth, but it gets powerfully practical and straightforward about how money is made. The wicked get it quick and easy. The god "Mammon" gives them a false sense of security, friends, and influence, but fails to mention the worry, pretense, and cutthroat competition that destroy all genuine relationships. Easy money is never easy or lasting. The godly individual recognizes that both rich and poor owe their existence to God. Money is one of His good gifts to be used as a trust from the Heavenly Father. "You cannot serve both God and Money!" (Matt. 6:24).

		REFERENCE NUMBERS
THE RICH AND INHERITANCES		

Bestowing

8:20-21   I walk in the way of righteousness, along the paths of justice, [21] **bestowing** wealth on those who love me and making their treasuries full.   5706

Inheritance

13:22   A good man leaves an **inheritance** for his children's children, but a sinner's wealth is stored up for the righteous.   5706

17:2   A wise servant will rule over a disgraceful son, and will share the **inheritance** as one of the brothers.   5709

19:14   Houses and wealth are **inherited** from parents, but a prudent wife is from the LORD.   5709

20:21   An **inheritance** quickly gained at the beginning will not be blessed at the end.   5709

THE RICH AND THE FEAR OF THE LORD

Rich

22:2   **Rich** and poor have this in common: The LORD is the Maker of them all.   6938

28:20   A faithful man will be richly blessed, but one eager to get **rich** will not go unpunished.   6947

Wealth

10:22   The blessing of the LORD brings **wealth**, and he adds no trouble to it.   6947

14:24   The **wealth** of the wise is their crown, but the folly of fools yields folly.   6948

22:4   Humility and the fear of the LORD bring **wealth** and honor and life.   6948

THE RICH AND GIVING

Wealth

3:9-10   Honor the LORD with your **wealth**, with the firstfruits of all your crops; [10] then your barns will be filled to overflowing, and your vats will brim over with new wine.   2104

THE PRACTICE OF WISDOM

THE RICH AND WORK

Abundant

28:19   He who works his land will have **abundant** food, but the one   8425
        who chases fantasies will have his fill of poverty.

Money

13:11   Dishonest **money** dwindles away, but he who gathers **money**   2104/NIH
        little by little makes it grow.

Profit

14:23   All hard work brings a **profit**, but mere talk leads only to pov-   4639
        erty.

21:5   The plans of the diligent lead to **profit** as surely as haste leads   4639
        to poverty.

Rich

23:4   Do not wear yourself out to get **rich**; have the wisdom to show   6947
        restraint.

Wealth

10:4   Lazy hands make a man poor, but diligent hands bring **wealth**.   6947

11:16   A kindhearted woman gains respect, but ruthless men gain only   6948
        wealth.

THE RICH AND WICKEDNESS

Rich

28:6   Better a poor man whose walk is blameless than a **rich** man   6938
        whose ways are perverse.

28:22   A stingy man is eager to get **rich** and is unaware that poverty   2104
        awaits him.

Treasures

10:2   Ill-gotten **treasures** are of no value, but righteousness delivers   238
        from death.

Wealth

11:4   **Wealth** is worthless in the day of wrath, but righteousness de-   2104
        livers from death.

THE RICH AND INFLUENCE

Rich

14:20   The poor are shunned even by their neighbors, but the **rich**   6938
        have many friends.

18:23   A poor man pleads for mercy, but a **rich** man answers harshly.   6938

Wealth

19:4   **Wealth** brings many friends, but a poor man's friend deserts   2104
        him.

THE RICH AND THE POOR

Rich

22:7   The **rich** rule over the poor, and the borrower is servant to the   6938
        lender.

22:16   He who oppresses the poor to increase his wealth and he who   6938
        gives gifts to the **rich**—both come to poverty.

THE RICH AND SECURITY

Rich

10:15   The wealth of the **rich** is their fortified city, but poverty is the   6938
        ruin of the poor.

		REFERENCE NUMBERS

| 18:11 | The wealth of the **rich** is their fortified city; they imagine it an unscalable wall. | 6938 |

Riches

| 13:8 | A man's **riches** may ransom his life, but a poor man hears no threat. | 6948 |

THE RICH AND INSECURITY

Rich

| 13:7 | One man pretends to be **rich**, yet has nothing; another pretends to be poor, yet has great wealth. | 6947 |
| 28:11 | A **rich** man may be wise in his own eyes, but a poor man who has discernment sees through him. | 6938 |

Riches

11:28	Whoever trusts in his **riches** will fall, but the righteous will thrive like a green leaf.	6948
23:5	Cast but a glance at **riches**, and they are gone, for they will surely sprout wings and fly off to the sky like an eagle.	2257s
27:24	for **riches** do not endure forever, and a crown is not secure for all generations.	2890

CONTRASTS TO THE RICH

Poor

10:4	Lazy hands make a man **poor**, but diligent hands bring wealth.	8133
10:15	The wealth of the rich is their fortified city, but poverty is the ruin of the **poor**.	1924
13:8	A man's riches may ransom his life, but a **poor** man hears no threat.	8133
14:20	The **poor** are shunned even by their neighbors, but the rich have many friends.	8133
18:23	A **poor** man pleads for mercy, but a rich man answers harshly.	8133
21:17	He who loves pleasure will become **poor**; whoever loves wine and oil will never be rich.	4728

Poverty

14:23	All hard work brings a profit, but mere talk leads only to **poverty**.	4728
21:5	The plans of the diligent lead to profit as surely as haste leads to **poverty**.	4728
28:19	He who works his land will have abundant food, but the one who chases fantasies will have his fill of **poverty**.	8203

RICHES

Recognizing the control material things can have over our lives, Proverbs uses an assortment of analogies comparing earthly riches to eternal values to motivate us to escape the money trap. God does His accounting in hearts, not in spread sheets. Knowledge, wisdom, a faithful marriage partner—these are a few of the riches in life worth the investment. The intensity with which men and women pursue money should be invested in cultivating their relationships with their Creator. On planet Earth there are only two things that are eternal—God's Word and human beings. The wise individual invests his life in both.

		REFERENCE NUMBERS
RICHES AND THE TONGUE		
Fortune		
21:6	A **fortune** made by a lying tongue is a fleeting vapor and a deadly snare.	238
Glaze		
26:23	Like a coating of **glaze** over earthenware are fervent lips with an evil heart.	6213
Gold		
20:15	**Gold** there is, and rubies in abundance, but lips that speak knowledge are a rare jewel.	2298
25:11	A word aptly spoken is like apples of **gold** in settings of silver.	2298
Silver		
10:20	The tongue of the righteous is choice **silver**, but the heart of the wicked is of little value.	4084
RICHES AND DISCIPLINE		
Gold		
17:3	The crucible for silver and the furnace for **gold**, but the Lord tests the heart.	2298
25:12	Like an earring of **gold** or an ornament of fine **gold** is a wise man's rebuke to a listening ear.	2298/4188
27:21	The crucible for silver and the furnace for **gold**, but man is tested by the praise he receives.	2298
Silver		
25:4-5	Remove the dross from the **silver**, and out comes material for the silversmith; [5] remove the wicked from the king's presence, and his throne will be established through righteousness.	4084
RICHES AND WISDOM		
Gold		
3:13-15	Blessed is the man who finds wisdom, the man who gains understanding, [14] for she is more profitable than silver and yields better returns than **gold**. [15] She is more precious than rubies; nothing you desire can compare with her.	3021
8:10	Choose my instruction instead of silver, knowledge rather than choice **gold**,	3021
8:19	My fruit is better than fine **gold**; what I yield surpasses choice silver.	7058
16:16	How much better to get wisdom than **gold**, to choose understanding rather than silver!	3021

Oil

21:20   In the house of the wise are stores of choice food and **oil**, but a   9043
foolish man devours all he has.

Treasure

2:1-5   My son, if you accept my words and store up my commands   4759
within you, [2] turning your ear to wisdom and applying your
heart to understanding, [3] and if you call out for insight and
cry aloud for understanding, [4] and if you look for it as for silver and search for it as for hidden **treasure**, [5] then you will
understand the fear of the LORD and find the knowledge of
God.

RICHES AND VIRTUE

Rubies

31:10   A wife of noble character who can find? She is worth far more   7165
than **rubies**.

RICHES AND THE FEAR OF THE LORD

Treasure

15:6   The house of the righteous contains great **treasure**, but the in-   2890
come of the wicked brings them trouble.

Wealth

3:9   Honor the LORD with your **wealth**, with the firstfruits of all   2104
your crops;

8:21   bestowing **wealth** on those who love me and making their trea-   3780
suries full.

RICHES AND THE WICKED

Treasures

10:2   Ill-gotten **treasures** are of no value, but righteousness delivers   238
from death.

Wealth

6:30-31   Men do not despise a thief if he steals to satisfy his hunger   2104
when he is starving. [31] Yet if he is caught, he must pay sevenfold, though it costs him all the **wealth** of his house.

28:8   He who increases his **wealth** by exorbitant interest amasses it   2104
for another, who will be kind to the poor.

29:3   A man who loves wisdom brings joy to his father, but a com-   2104
panion of prostitutes squanders his **wealth**.

RIGHTEOUSNESS

Proverbs assumes that moral standards exist and that God has revealed them. Throughout the book righteousness and wickedness struggle. Those who trust the Designer and obey His blueprint find life, whereas those who reject His plan deny reality and, though they may prosper for a time, ultimately face destruction. Many of society's calamities result from a flagrant rejection of God's will. Righteousness—obedience to God's standards—does yield life, yet only one man ever earned the right to enter God's presence based on obedience. Amazingly this Savior graciously offers His righteousness to anyone who will believe Him. "He saved us, not because of righteous things we had done, but because of his mercy" (Titus 3:5).

RIGHTEOUSNESS AND BLESSINGS		REFERENCE NUMBERS
Righteous		
3:33	The Lord's curse is on the house of the wicked, but he blesses the home of the **righteous**.	7404
10:6-7	Blessings crown the head of the **righteous**, but violence overwhelms the mouth of the wicked. [7] The memory of the **righteous** will be a blessing, but the name of the wicked will rot.	7404/7404
10:24-25	What the wicked dreads will overtake him; what the **righteous** desire will be granted. [25] When the storm has swept by, the wicked are gone, but the **righteous** stand firm forever.	7404/7404
10:28	The prospect of the **righteous** is joy, but the hopes of the wicked come to nothing.	7404
11:10	When the **righteous** prosper, the city rejoices; when the wicked perish, there are shouts of joy.	7404
11:28	Whoever trusts in his riches will fall, but the **righteous** will thrive like a green leaf.	7404
12:12	The wicked desire the plunder of evil men, but the root of the **righteous** flourishes.	7404
13:9	The light of the **righteous** shines brightly, but the lamp of the wicked is snuffed out.	7404
13:21-22	Misfortune pursues the sinner, but prosperity is the reward of the **righteous**. [22] A good man leaves an inheritance for his children's children, but a sinner's wealth is stored up for the **righteous**.	7404/7404
13:25	The **righteous** eat to their hearts' content, but the stomach of the wicked goes hungry.	7404
15:6	The house of the **righteous** contains great treasure, but the income of the wicked brings them trouble.	7404
20:7	The **righteous** man leads a blameless life; blessed are his children after him.	7404
23:24	The father of a **righteous** man has great joy; he who has a wise son delights in him.	7404
28:12	When the **righteous** triumph, there is great elation; but when the wicked rise to power, men go into hiding.	7404
29:2	When the **righteous** thrive, the people rejoice; when the wicked rule, the people groan.	7404
29:6	An evil man is snared by his own sin, but a **righteous** one can sing and be glad.	7404

Righteousness

14:34	**Righteousness** exalts a nation, but sin is a disgrace to any people.	7407
16:8	Better a little with **righteousness** than much gain with injustice.	7407
21:21	He who pursues **righteousness** and love finds life, prosperity and honor.	7407

Upright

3:32	for the LORD detests a perverse man but takes the **upright** into his confidence.	3838
11:11	Through the blessing of the **upright** a city is exalted, but by the mouth of the wicked it is destroyed.	3838
14:9	Fools mock at making amends for sin, but goodwill is found among the **upright**.	3838
14:11	The house of the wicked will be destroyed, but the tent of the **upright** will flourish.	3838
28:10	He who leads the **upright** along an evil path will fall into his own trap, but the blameless will receive a good inheritance.	3838

RIGHTEOUSNESS AND LEARNING

Right

8:6	Listen, for I have worthy things to say; I open my lips to speak what is **right**.	4797
8:9	To the discerning all of them are **right**; they are faultless to those who have knowledge.	5791

Righteous

2:20	Thus you will walk in the ways of good men and keep to the paths of the **righteous**.	7404
9:9	Instruct a wise man and he will be wiser still; teach a **righteous** man and he will add to his learning.	7404
11:9	With his mouth the godless destroys his neighbor, but through knowledge the **righteous** escape.	7404

Upright

15:19	The way of the sluggard is blocked with thorns, but the path of the **upright** is a highway.	3838

RIGHTEOUSNESS AND THE TONGUE

Just

8:8	All the words of my mouth are **just**; none of them is crooked or perverse.	7406

Righteous

10:11	The mouth of the **righteous** is a fountain of life, but violence overwhelms the mouth of the wicked.	7404
10:21	The lips of the **righteous** nourish many, but fools die for lack of judgment.	7404
10:31-32	The mouth of the **righteous** brings forth wisdom, but a perverse tongue will be cut out. [32] The lips of the **righteous** know what is fitting, but the mouth of the wicked only what is perverse.	7404/7404
12:13	An evil man is trapped by his sinful talk, but a **righteous** man escapes trouble.	7404
15:28	The heart of the **righteous** weighs its answers, but the mouth of the wicked gushes evil.	7404

		REFERENCE NUMBERS
28:1	The wicked man flees though no one pursues, but the **righteous** are as bold as a lion.	7404

RIGHTEOUSNESS AND PROTECTION

Righteous

10:3	The LORD does not let the **righteous** go hungry but he thwarts the craving of the wicked.	7404
10:29	The way of the LORD is a refuge for the **righteous**, but it is the ruin of those who do evil.	9448
11:8	The **righteous** man is rescued from trouble, and it comes on the wicked instead.	7404
11:21	Be sure of this: The wicked will not go unpunished, but those who are **righteous** will go free.	2446 + 7404
12:3	A man cannot be established through wickedness, but the **righteous** cannot be uprooted.	7404
12:7	Wicked men are overthrown and are no more, but the house of the **righteous** stands firm.	7404
12:21	No harm befalls the **righteous**, but the wicked have their fill of trouble.	7404
18:10	The name of the LORD is a strong tower; the **righteous** run to it and are safe.	7404
24:15-16	Do not lie in wait like an outlaw against a **righteous** man's house, do not raid his dwelling place; [16] for though a **righteous** man falls seven times, he rises again, but the wicked are brought down by calamity.	7404/7404

Righteousness

10:2	Ill-gotten treasures are of no value, but **righteousness** delivers from death.	7407
11:4-6	Wealth is worthless in the day of wrath, but **righteousness** delivers from death. [5] The **righteousness** of the blameless makes a straight way for them, but the wicked are brought down by their own wickedness. [6] The **righteousness** of the upright delivers them, but the unfaithful are trapped by evil desires.	7407/7407/7407
13:6	**Righteousness** guards the man of integrity, but wickedness overthrows the sinner.	7407

Upright

2:7-8	He holds victory in store for the **upright**, he is a shield to those whose walk is blameless, [8] for he guards the course of the just and protects the way of his faithful ones.	3838
29:10	Bloodthirsty men hate a man of integrity and seek to kill the **upright**.	3838

RIGHTEOUSNESS AND JUSTICE

Innocent

17:15	Acquitting the guilty and condemning the **innocent**—the LORD detests them both.	7404
18:5	It is not good to be partial to the wicked or to deprive the **innocent** of justice.	7404

Right

18:17	The first to present his case seems **right**, till another comes forward and questions him.	7404
25:26	Like a muddied spring or a polluted well is a **righteous** man who gives way to the wicked.	7404

Righteous

11:31   If the **righteous** receive their due on earth, how much more the   7404
ungodly and the sinner!

13:5   The **righteous** hate what is false, but the wicked bring shame   7404
and disgrace.

21:15   When justice is done, it brings joy to the **righteous** but terror to   7404
evildoers.

Righteousness

8:20   I walk in the way of **righteousness**, along the paths of justice,   7407

16:12   Kings detest wrongdoing, for a throne is established through   7407
righteousness.

RIGHTEOUSNESS AND LIFE

Righteous

11:19   The truly **righteous** man attains life, but he who pursues evil   7407
goes to his death.

11:30   The fruit of the **righteous** is a tree of life, and he who wins   7404
souls is wise.

14:32   When calamity comes, the wicked are brought down, but even   7404
in death the **righteous** have a refuge.

Righteousness

12:28   In the way of **righteousness** there is life; along that path is im-   7407
mortality.

RIGHTEOUSNESS AND WORK

Righteousness

11:18   The wicked man earns deceptive wages, but he who sows **righ-**   7407
teousness reaps a sure reward.

RIGHTEOUSNESS AND THE FEAR OF THE LORD

Blameless

11:20   The LORD detests men of perverse heart but he delights in those   9459
whose ways are **blameless**.

Righteous

15:29   The LORD is far from the wicked but he hears the prayer of the   7404
righteous.

Righteousness

15:9   The LORD detests the way of the wicked but he loves those who   7407
pursue **righteousness**.

Upright

14:2   He whose walk is **upright** fears the LORD, but he whose ways   3841
are devious despises him.

15:8   The LORD detests the sacrifice of the wicked, but the prayer of   3838
the **upright** pleases him.

RIGHTEOUSNESS AND GIVING

Righteous

21:25-26 The sluggard's craving will be the death of him, because his   7404
hands refuse to work. [26] All day long he craves for more, but
the **righteous** give without sparing.

29:7   The **righteous** care about justice for the poor, but the wicked   7404
have no such concern.

THE PRACTICE OF WISDOM

RIGHTEOUSNESS AND AUTHORITIES

Righteous
29:2   When the **righteous** thrive, the people rejoice; when the wick-   7404
        ed rule, the people groan.

Righteousness
16:12   Kings detest wrongdoing, for a throne is established through   7407
        righteousness.

25:4-5 Remove the dross from the silver, and out comes material for   7406
        the silversmith; [5] remove the wicked from the king's pres-
        ence, and his throne will be established through **righteousness.**

TIMES OF TROUBLE

Because we reside in a fallen world, all of us experience hard times, both deserved and undeserved. Meddling, hot-headedness, greed, garrulousness, lying, rebellion, and addiction—Proverbs honestly guarantees this kind of behavior will get us in trouble. When we deserve it, affliction is understandable. The tough questions come when we, or a loved one, become an innocent victim. Does rebellious anger against God meet our need in these hard times? Job gives us the right to be honest emotionally and spiritually before God and to learn how affliction can draw us near to the Father. Proverbs reveals the character traits He can generate in the midst of unexplainable difficulties —kindness, friendship, righteousness, faithfulness, wisdom, and teachability to realize that "in all things God works for the good of those who love him, who have been called according to his purpose" (Rom. 8:28).

TIMES OF TROUBLE RELATED TO AFFLICTION		REFERENCE NUMBERS
Adversity		
17:17	A friend loves at all times, and a brother is born for **adversity**.	7650
Calamity		
1:24-27	But since you rejected me when I called and no one gave heed when I stretched out my hand, [25] since you ignored all my advice and would not accept my rebuke, [26] I in turn will laugh at your disaster; I will mock when **calamity** overtakes you—[27] when **calamity** overtakes you like a storm, when disaster sweeps over you like a whirlwind, when distress and trouble overwhelm you.	7065/7065
Oppressed		
15:15	All the days of the **oppressed** are wretched, but the cheerful heart has a continual feast.	6714
Quarrel		
17:14	Starting a **quarrel** is like breaching a dam; so drop the matter before a dispute breaks out.	4506
26:17	Like one who seizes a dog by the ears is a passer-by who meddles in a **quarrel** not his own.	8190
Quarrelsome		
26:21	As charcoal to embers and as wood to fire, so is a **quarrelsome** man for kindling strife.	4506
Shame		
25:6-8	Do not exalt yourself in the king's presence, and do not claim a place among great men; [7] it is better for him to say to you, "Come up here," than for him to humiliate you before a nobleman. What you have seen with your eyes [8] do not bring hastily to court, for what will you do in the end if your neighbor puts you to **shame**?	4007
Strife		
17:1	Better a dry crust with peace and quiet than a house full of feasting, with **strife**.	8190
30:33	"For as churning the milk produces butter, and as twisting the nose produces blood, so stirring up anger produces **strife**."	8190
Trouble		
11:17	A kind man benefits himself, but a cruel man brings **trouble** on himself.	6579
11:29	He who brings **trouble** on his family will inherit only wind, and the fool will be servant to the wise.	6579

		REFERENCE NUMBERS
15:27	A greedy man brings **trouble** to his family, but he who hates bribes will live.	6579
24:10	If you falter in times of **trouble**, how small is your strength!	7650
25:19	Like a bad tooth or a lame foot is reliance on the unfaithful in times of **trouble**.	7650

Turmoil

| 15:16 | Better a little with the fear of the LORD than great wealth with **turmoil**. | 4539 |

TIMES OF TROUBLE RELATED TO THE POOR

Crush

| 22:22 | Do not exploit the poor because they are poor and do not **crush** the needy in court, | 1608 |

TIMES OF TROUBLE RELATED TO THE TONGUE

Calamity

| 21:23 | He who guards his mouth and his tongue keeps himself from **calamity**. | 7650 |

Dissension

| 16:28 | A perverse man stirs up **dissension**, and a gossip separates close friends. | 4506 |

Hurts

| 26:28 | A lying tongue hates those it **hurts**, and a flattering mouth works ruin. | 1916 |

Quarrel

| 26:20 | Without wood a fire goes out; without gossip a **quarrel** dies down. | 4506 |

Trapped

| 12:13 | An evil man is **trapped** by his sinful talk, but a righteous man escapes trouble. | 4613 |

TIMES OF TROUBLE RELATED TO GOD'S PROTECTION

Fear

| 3:25 | Have no **fear** of sudden disaster or of the ruin that overtakes the wicked, | 3707 |

Rescued

| 11:8 | The righteous man is **rescued** from trouble, and it comes on the wicked instead. | 2740 |

Safe

| 29:25 | Fear of man will prove to be a snare, but whoever trusts in the LORD is kept **safe**. | 8435 |

Safety

| 1:33 | "but whoever listens to me will live in **safety** and be at ease, without fear of harm." | 1055 |

Seek

| 28:5 | Evil men do not understand justice, but those who **seek** the LORD understand it fully. | 1335 |

Shuns

| 14:16 | A wise man fears the LORD and **shuns** evil, but a fool is hot-headed and reckless. | 6073 |

TIMES OF TROUBLE RELATED TO THE WICKED

Dissension
16:28   A perverse man stirs up **dissension**, and a gossip separates   4506
close friends.

28:25   A greedy man stirs up **dissension**, but he who trusts in the   4506
Lord will prosper.

Dreads
10:24   What the wicked **dreads** will overtake him; what the righteous   4475
desire will be granted.

Quarrel
17:19   He who loves a **quarrel** loves sin; he who builds a high gate   5175
invites destruction.

Scorn
13:13   He who **scorns** instruction will pay for it, but he who respects a   996
command is rewarded.

Trouble
15:6   The house of the righteous contains great treasure, but the in-   6579
come of the wicked brings them **trouble**.

Wicked
25:26   Like a muddied spring or a polluted well is a righteous man   8401
who gives way to the **wicked**.

TIMES OF TROUBLE RELATED TO AUTHORITIES

Groan
29:2   When the righteous thrive, the people rejoice; when the wicked   634
rule, the people **groan**.

Rebellious
24:21   Fear the Lord and the king, my son, and do not join with the   9101
rebellious,

Wrath
20:2   A king's **wrath** is like the roar of a lion; he who angers him   399
forfeits his life.

TIMES OF TROUBLE RELATED TO DISCOURAGEMENT

Grief
14:13   Even in laughter the heart may ache, and joy may end in **grief**.   9342

Heartache
15:13   A happy heart makes the face cheerful, but **heartache** crushes   4213 + 6780
the spirit.

TIMES OF TROUBLE RELATED TO ALCOHOL

Anguish
31:5-7   lest they drink and forget what the law decrees, and deprive all   5253 + 5883
the oppressed of their rights. [6] Give beer to those who are
perishing, wine to those who are in **anguish**; [7] let them drink
and forget their poverty and remember their misery no more.

Sorrow
23:29-30   Who has woe? Who has **sorrow**? Who has strife? Who has   16
complaints? Who has needless bruises? Who has bloodshot
eyes? [30] Those who linger over wine, who go to sample
bowls of mixed wine.

		REFERENCE
TIMES OF TROUBLE RELATED TO THE FOOL		NUMBERS

Grief

17:21   To have a fool for a son brings **grief**; there is no joy for the   9342
father of a fool.

Quarrel

20:3   It is to a man's honor to avoid strife, but every fool is quick to   1679
quarrel.

22:10   Drive out the mocker, and out goes strife; **quarrels** and insults   1907
are ended.

Reckless

14:16   A wise man fears the LORD and shuns evil, but a fool is hot-   1053
headed and **reckless**.

Ruin

10:10   He who winks maliciously causes grief, and a chattering fool   4231
comes to **ruin**.

TIMES OF TROUBLE RELATED TO ANGER

Dissension

10:12   Hatred stirs up **dissension**, but love covers over all wrongs.   4506

15:18   A hot-tempered man stirs up **dissension**, but a patient man   4506
calms a quarrel.

29:22   An angry man stirs up **dissension**, and a hot-tempered one   4506
commits many sins.

Hot-Tempered

19:19   A **hot-tempered** man must pay the penalty; if you rescue him,   1524 + 2779
you will have to do it again.

THE TONGUE

When to speak and when to keep silent—the wise learn the art of skillful communication. They respect the sharpness of the sword in their mouth. Not only do fools wag their tongues indiscriminately, they also lie, plot, ambush, and destroy with words. Wise people use speech honestly, thoughtfully, gently, and truthfully. Only God's words are always true, and only those will endure. Let's enroll in God's speech class. Because of the tongue's great potential for good or evil (James 3:9), divine focus on the tongue should come as no surprise.

THE TONGUE AND DISCRETION (DISCERNMENT)		REFERENCE NUMBERS
Answer		
15:1	A gentle **answer** turns away wrath, but a harsh word stirs up anger.	5101
15:28	The heart of the righteous weighs its **answers**, but the mouth of the wicked gushes evil.	6699
18:13	He who **answers** before listening—that is his folly and his shame.	1821 + 8740
22:20-21	Have I not written thirty sayings for you, sayings of counsel and knowledge, [21] teaching you true and reliable words, so that you can give sound **answers** to him who sent you?	609
24:26	An honest **answer** is like a kiss on the lips.	1821 + 8740
26:4-5	Do not **answer** a fool according to his folly, or you will be like him yourself. [5] **Answer** a fool according to his folly, or he will be wise in his own eyes.	6699/6699
Lips		
5:1-2	My son, pay attention to my wisdom, listen well to my words of insight, [2] that you may maintain discretion and your **lips** may preserve knowledge.	8557
12:14	From the fruit of his **lips** a man is filled with good things as surely as the work of his hands rewards him.	7023
13:2-3	From the fruit of his **lips** a man enjoys good things, but the unfaithful have a craving for violence. [3] He who guards his **lips** guards his life, but he who speaks rashly will come to ruin.	7023/7023
16:23	A wise man's heart guides his mouth, and his **lips** promote instruction.	8557
18:20	From the fruit of his mouth a man's stomach is filled; with the harvest from his **lips** he is satisfied.	8557
22:17-18	Pay attention and listen to the sayings of the wise; apply your heart to what I teach, [18] for it is pleasing when you keep them in your heart and have all of them ready on your **lips**.	8557
23:15-16	My son, if your heart is wise, then my heart will be glad; [16] my inmost being will rejoice when your **lips** speak what is right.	8557
24:28	Do not testify against your neighbor without cause, or use your **lips** to deceive.	8557
27:2	Let another praise you, and not your own mouth; someone else, and not your own **lips**.	8557
Mouth		
18:4	The words of a man's **mouth** are deep waters, but the fountain of wisdom is a bubbling brook.	7023

Plans
16:1	To man belong the **plans** of the heart, but from the LORD comes the reply of the tongue.	5119

Speaks
29:20	Do you see a man who **speaks** in haste? There is more hope for a fool than for him.	1821

Tongue
10:19	When words are many, sin is not absent, but he who holds his **tongue** is wise.	8557
15:4	The **tongue** that brings healing is a tree of life, but a deceitful **tongue** crushes the spirit.	4383/2023s
17:28	Even a fool is thought wise if he keeps silent, and discerning if he holds his **tongue**.	8557
18:21	The **tongue** has the power of life and death, and those who love it will eat its fruit.	4383
25:15	Through patience a ruler can be persuaded, and a gentle **tongue** can break a bone.	4383

Words
17:27	A man of knowledge uses **words** with restraint, and a man of understanding is even-tempered.	609

THE TONGUE AND THE WICKED

Lips
16:30	He who winks with his eye is plotting perversity; he who purses his **lips** is bent on evil.	8557
17:4	A wicked man listens to evil **lips**; a liar pays attention to a malicious tongue.	8557
24:1-2	Do not envy wicked men, do not desire their company; [2] for their hearts plot violence, and their **lips** talk about making trouble.	8557
26:23	Like a coating of glaze over earthenware are fervent **lips** with an evil heart.	8557

Mouth
6:12-15	A scoundrel and villain, who goes about with a corrupt **mouth**, [13] who winks with his eye, signals with his feet and motions with his fingers, [14] who plots evil with deceit in his heart—he always stirs up dissension. [15] Therefore disaster will overtake him in an instant; he will suddenly be destroyed—without remedy.	7023
10:6	Blessings crown the head of the righteous, but violence overwhelms the **mouth** of the wicked.	7023
10:11	The **mouth** of the righteous is a fountain of life, but violence overwhelms the **mouth** of the wicked.	7023
10:32	The lips of the righteous know what is fitting, but the **mouth** of the wicked only what is perverse.	7023
11:9	With his **mouth** the godless destroys his neighbor, but through knowledge the righteous escape.	7023
11:11	Through the blessing of the upright a city is exalted, but by the **mouth** of the wicked it is destroyed.	7023
15:28	The heart of the righteous weighs its answers, but the **mouth** of the wicked gushes evil.	7023
19:28	A corrupt witness mocks at justice, and the **mouth** of the wicked gulps down evil.	7023

Speech
16:27 A scoundrel plots evil, and his **speech** is like a scorching fire. 8557

Talk
12:13 An evil man is trapped by his sinful **talk**, but a righteous man escapes trouble. 8557

Thoughts
15:26 The LORD detests the **thoughts** of the wicked, but those of the pure are pleasing to him. 4742

Tongue
10:31 The mouth of the righteous brings forth wisdom, but a perverse **tongue** will be cut out. 4383

15:4 The **tongue** that brings healing is a tree of life, but a deceitful **tongue** crushes the spirit. 4383/2023s

17:20 A man of perverse heart does not prosper; he whose **tongue** is deceitful falls into trouble. 4383

Words
12:6 The **words** of the wicked lie in wait for blood, but the speech of the upright rescues them. 1821

22:12 The eyes of the LORD keep watch over knowledge, but he frustrates the **words** of the unfaithful. 1821

THE TONGUE AND THE RIGHTEOUS

Answers
15:28 The heart of the righteous weighs its **answers**, but the mouth of the wicked gushes evil. 6699

Lips
10:21 The **lips** of the righteous nourish many, but fools die for lack of judgment. 8557

10:32 The **lips** of the righteous know what is fitting, but the mouth of the wicked only what is perverse. 8557

16:13 Kings take pleasure in honest **lips**; they value a man who speaks the truth. 8557

Mouth
10:11 The **mouth** of the righteous is a fountain of life, but violence overwhelms the **mouth** of the wicked. 7023

10:31 The **mouth** of the righteous brings forth wisdom, but a perverse tongue will be cut out. 7023

Speak
31:8-9 "**Speak** up for those who cannot **speak** for themselves, for the rights of all who are destitute. [9] **Speak** up and judge fairly; defend the rights of the poor and needy." 7023 + 7337/ 522/ 7023 + 7337

Speech
12:6 The words of the wicked lie in wait for blood, but the **speech** of the upright rescues them. 7023

Tongue
10:20 The **tongue** of the righteous is choice silver, but the heart of the wicked is of little value. 4383

THE TONGUE AND TRUTH

Lips
8:6-8 Listen, for I have worthy things to say; I open my **lips** to speak what is right. [7] My mouth speaks what is true, for my **lips** detest wickedness. [8] All the words of my mouth are just; none of them is crooked or perverse. 8557/8557

12:19 Truthful **lips** endure forever, but a lying tongue lasts only a moment. 8557

Sayings

22:20-21 Have I not written thirty **sayings** for you, **sayings** of counsel and knowledge, [21] teaching you true and reliable words, so that you can give sound answers to him who sent you? NIH/NIH

Testimony

12:17 A truthful witness gives honest **testimony**, but a false witness tells lies. 5583

Witness

14:25 A truthful **witness** saves lives, but a false **witness** is deceitful. 6332/7032

Words

30:5-6 "Every word of God is flawless; he is a shield to those who take refuge in him. [6] Do not add to his **words**, or he will rebuke you and prove you a liar." 614/1821

THE TONGUE AND THE FOOL

Answer

26:4-5 Do not **answer** a fool according to his folly, or you will be like him yourself. [5] **Answer** a fool according to his folly, or he will be wise in his own eyes. 6699/6699

Hearts

15:7 The lips of the wise spread knowledge; not so the **hearts** of fools. 4213

Lips

14:7 Stay away from a foolish man, for you will not find knowledge on his **lips**. 8557

17:7 Arrogant **lips** are unsuited to a fool—how much worse lying **lips** to a ruler! 8557/8557

18:6-7 A fool's **lips** bring him strife, and his mouth invites a beating. [7] A fool's mouth is his undoing, and his **lips** are a snare to his soul. 8557/8557

19:1 Better a poor man whose walk is blameless than a fool whose **lips** are perverse. 8557

Mouth

10:14 Wise men store up knowledge, but the **mouth** of a fool invites ruin. 7023

15:2 The tongue of the wise commends knowledge, but the **mouth** of the fool gushes folly. 7023

15:14 The discerning heart seeks knowledge, but the **mouth** of a fool feeds on folly. 7023

26:7 Like a lame man's legs that hang limp is a proverb in the **mouth** of a fool. 7023

26:9 Like a thornbush in a drunkard's hand is a proverb in the **mouth** of a fool. 7023

Slander

10:18 He who conceals his hatred has lying lips, and whoever spreads **slander** is a fool. 1804

Speak

13:3 He who guards his lips guards his life, but he who **speaks** rashly will come to ruin. 7316 + 8557

23:9 Do not **speak** to a fool, for he will scorn the wisdom of your words. 1819

Talk

14:3   A fool's **talk** brings a rod to his back, but the lips of the wise   7023
protect them.

Tongue

17:28   Even a fool is thought wise if he keeps silent, and discerning if   8557
he holds his **tongue**.

THE TONGUE AND THE WISE

Answer

27:11   Be wise, my son, and bring joy to my heart; then I can **answer**   1821 + 8740
anyone who treats me with contempt.

Lips

10:13   Wisdom is found on the **lips** of the discerning, but a rod is for   8557
the back of him who lacks judgment.

14:3   A fool's talk brings a rod to his back, but the **lips** of the wise   8557
protect them.

15:7   The **lips** of the wise spread knowledge; not so the hearts of   8557
fools.

20:15   Gold there is, and rubies in abundance, but **lips** that speak   8557
knowledge are a rare jewel.

Mouth

16:23   A wise man's heart guides his **mouth**, and his lips promote in-   7023
struction.

18:4   The words of a man's **mouth** are deep waters, but the fountain   7023
of wisdom is a bubbling brook.

Sayings

22:17-18 Pay attention and listen to the **sayings** of the wise; apply your   1821
heart to what I teach, [18] for it is pleasing when you keep them
in your heart and have all of them ready on your lips.

Tongue

10:19   When words are many, sin is not absent, but he who holds his   8557
tongue is wise.

12:18   Reckless words pierce like a sword, but the **tongue** of the wise   4383
brings healing.

15:2   The **tongue** of the wise commends knowledge, but the mouth   4383
of the fool gushes folly.

31:26   She speaks with wisdom, and faithful instruction is on her   4383
tongue.

Words

4:3-5   When I was a boy in my father's house, still tender, and an   1821/609
only child of my mother, [4] he taught me and said, "Lay hold   + 7023
of my **words** with all your heart; keep my commands and you
will live. [5] Get wisdom, get understanding; do not forget my
words or swerve from them."

16:21   The wise in heart are called discerning, and pleasant **words**   8557
promote instruction.

THE TONGUE AND LYING

Deceives

26:19   is a man who **deceives** his neighbor and says, "I was only jok-   8228
ing!"

False Witness

12:17   A truthful witness gives honest testimony, but a **false witness**   9214/6332
tells lies.

		REFERENCE NUMBERS
14:25	A truthful witness saves lives, but a **false witness** is deceitful.	3942/7032
19:5	A **false witness** will not go unpunished, and he who pours out lies will not go free.	9214/6332
19:9	A **false witness** will not go unpunished, and he who pours out lies will perish.	9214/6332
21:28	A **false witness** will perish, and whoever listens to him will be destroyed forever.	3942/6332

Lips

10:18	He who conceals his hatred has lying **lips**, and whoever spreads slander is a fool.	8557
12:22	The Lᴏʀᴅ detests lying **lips**, but he delights in men who are truthful.	8557
17:7	Arrogant **lips** are unsuited to a fool—how much worse lying **lips** to a ruler!	8557/8557
26:24-25	A malicious man disguises himself with his **lips**, but in his heart he harbors deceit. [25] Though his speech is charming, do not believe him, for seven abominations fill his heart.	8557

Tongue

6:16-19	There are six things the Lᴏʀᴅ hates, seven that are detestable to him: [17] haughty eyes, a lying **tongue**, hands that shed innocent blood, [18] a heart that devises wicked schemes, feet that are quick to rush into evil, [19] a false witness who pours out lies and a man who stirs up dissension among brothers.	4383
12:19	Truthful lips endure forever, but a lying **tongue** lasts only a moment.	4383
17:4	A wicked man listens to evil lips; a liar pays attention to a malicious **tongue**.	4383
21:6	A fortune made by a lying **tongue** is a fleeting vapor and a deadly snare.	4383
26:28	A lying **tongue** hates those it hurts, and a flattering mouth works ruin.	4383

THE TONGUE AND DISCIPLINE

Rebukes

28:23	He who **rebukes** a man will in the end gain more favor than he who has a flattering tongue.	3519

Tongue

25:23	As a north wind brings rain, so a sly **tongue** brings angry looks.	4383

Words

29:19	A servant cannot be corrected by mere **words**; though he understands, he will not respond.	1821

THE TONGUE AND INSTRUCTION

Command

13:13	He who scorns instruction will pay for it, but he who respects a **command** is rewarded.	5184

Lips

4:24	Put away perversity from your mouth; keep corrupt talk far from your **lips**.	8557
8:6	Listen, for I have worthy things to say; I open my **lips** to speak what is right.	8557
14:7	Stay away from a foolish man, for you will not find knowledge on his **lips**.	8557

		REFERENCE NUMBERS
22:17-18	Pay attention and listen to the sayings of the wise; apply your heart to what I teach, [18] for it is pleasing when you keep them in your heart and have all of them ready on your **lips**.	8557

Say

4:10	Listen, my son, accept what I **say**, and the years of your life will be many.	609
4:20	My son, pay attention to what I **say**; listen closely to my words.	1821

Words

7:1-5	My son, keep my **words** and store up my commands within you. [2] Keep my commands and you will live; guard my teachings as the apple of your eye. [3] Bind them on your fingers; write them on the tablet of your heart. [4] Say to wisdom, "You are my sister," and call understanding your kinsman; [5] they will keep you from the adulteress, from the wayward wife with her seductive **words**.	609/609
19:27	Stop listening to instruction, my son, and you will stray from the **words** of knowledge.	609
23:12	Apply your heart to instruction and your ears to **words** of knowledge.	609

THE TONGUE AND IMMORALITY

Lips

5:3-4	For the **lips** of an adulteress drip honey, and her speech is smoother than oil; [4] but in the end she is bitter as gall, sharp as a double-edged sword.	8557

Mouth

22:14	The **mouth** of an adulteress is a deep pit; he who is under the Lord's wrath will fall into it.	7023
30:20	"This is the way of an adulteress: She eats and wipes her **mouth** and says, 'I've done nothing wrong.' "	7023

Tongue

6:24	keeping you from the immoral woman, from the smooth **tongue** of the wayward wife.	4383

Words

2:16	It will save you also from the adulteress, from the wayward wife with her seductive **words**,	609
7:5	they will keep you from the adulteress, from the wayward wife with her seductive **words**.	609
7:21	With persuasive **words** she led him astray; she seduced him with her smooth talk.	4375

THE TONGUE AND GOSSIP

Flatters

29:5	Whoever **flatters** his neighbor is spreading a net for his feet.	2744

Gossip

11:13	A **gossip** betrays a confidence, but a trustworthy man keeps a secret.	2143 + 8215
16:28	A perverse man stirs up dissension, and a **gossip** separates close friends.	8087
18:8	The words of a **gossip** are like choice morsels; they go down to a man's inmost parts.	8087
20:19	A **gossip** betrays a confidence; so avoid a man who talks too much.	2143 + 8215
26:20	Without wood a fire goes out; without **gossip** a quarrel dies down.	8087

REFERENCE
NUMBERS

26:22   The words of a **gossip** are like choice morsels; they go down to   8087
a man's inmost parts.

Lips
24:28   Do not testify against your neighbor without cause, or use your   8557
lips to deceive.

Mouth
11:9   With his **mouth** the godless destroys his neighbor, but through   7023
knowledge the righteous escape.

26:28   A lying tongue hates those it hurts, and a flattering **mouth**   7023
works ruin.

Words
12:18   Reckless **words** pierce like a sword, but the tongue of the wise   1051
brings healing.

THE TONGUE AND HATRED

Lips
10:18   He who conceals his hatred has lying **lips**, and whoever spreads   8557
slander is a fool.

26:24-25 A malicious man disguises himself with his **lips**, but in his   8557
heart he harbors deceit. [25] Though his speech is charming, do
not believe him, for seven abominations fill his heart.

THE TONGUE AND WORK

Lips
12:14   From the fruit of his **lips** a man is filled with good things as   7023
surely as the work of his hands rewards him.

Talk
14:23   All hard work brings a profit, but mere **talk** leads only to pov-   1821 + 8557
erty.

THE TONGUE AND AUTHORITIES

Lips
16:10   The **lips** of a king speak as an oracle, and his mouth should not   8557
betray justice.

16:13   Kings take pleasure in honest **lips**; they value a man who   8557
speaks the truth.

Speech
22:11   He who loves a pure heart and whose **speech** is gracious will   8557
have the king for his friend.

Tongue
25:15   Through patience a ruler can be persuaded, and a gentle **tongue**   4383
can break a bone.

THE TONGUE AND ENCOURAGEMENT

Word
12:25   An anxious heart weighs a man down, but a kind **word** cheers   1821
him up.

15:23   A man finds joy in giving an apt reply—and how good is a   1821
timely **word**!

16:24   Pleasant **words** are a honeycomb, sweet to the soul and healing   609
to the bones.

25:11   A **word** aptly spoken is like apples of gold in settings of silver.   1821

THE TONGUE AND BOASTING

Boasts
    20:14   "It's no good, it's no good!" says the buyer; then off he goes   2146
             and **boasts** about his purchase.

Lips
    27:2   Let another praise you, and not your own mouth; someone else,   8557
             and not your own **lips**.

TRUTH

Along with wisdom, discipline, and discernment, truth is worth selling everything you own to possess. Truth can elevate us to the halls of power, but the powerful dare not forget its impartiality. Justice is truth in the courtroom. Honesty is truth in relationships. All Scripture is truth, and the truth will faithfully lead us to the Son of God. "Whoever lives by the truth comes into the light" (John 3:21).

TRUTH AND JUDGMENT		REFERENCE NUMBERS
Injustice		
13:23	A poor man's field may produce abundant food, but **injustice** sweeps it away.	4202 + 5477
Judging		
24:23-25	These also are sayings of the wise: To show partiality in **judging** is not good: [24] Whoever says to the guilty, "You are innocent"—peoples will curse him and nations denounce him. [25] But it will go well with those who convict the guilty, and rich blessing will come upon them.	5477
Just		
1:1-6	The proverbs of Solomon son of David, king of Israel: [2] for attaining wisdom and discipline; for understanding words of insight; [3] for acquiring a disciplined and prudent life, doing what is right and **just** and fair; [4] for giving prudence to the simple, knowledge and discretion to the young— [5] let the wise listen and add to their learning, and let the discerning get guidance—[6] for understanding proverbs and parables, the sayings and riddles of the wise.	5477
2:7-9	He holds victory in store for the upright, he is a shield to those whose walk is blameless, [8] for he guards the course of the **just** and protects the way of his faithful ones. [9] Then you will understand what is right and **just** and fair—every good path.	5477/5477
21:3	To do what is right and **just** is more acceptable to the LORD than sacrifice.	5477
Justice		
8:20	I walk in the way of righteousness, along the paths of **justice**,	5477
18:5	It is not good to be partial to the wicked or to deprive the innocent of **justice**.	5477
21:15	When **justice** is done, it brings joy to the righteous but terror to evildoers.	5477
Truth		
23:23	Buy the **truth** and do not sell it; get wisdom, discipline and understanding.	622

TRUTH AND AUTHORITIES

Faithfulness		
20:28	Love and **faithfulness** keep a king safe; through love his throne is made secure.	622
Judge		
20:8	When a king sits on his throne to **judge**, he winnows out all evil with his eyes.	1907
Just		
8:15	By me kings reign and rulers make laws that are **just**;	7406

Justice

16:10 The lips of a king speak as an oracle, and his mouth should not betray **justice**. 5477

29:4 By **justice** a king gives a country stability, but one who is greedy for bribes tears it down. 5477

29:7 The righteous care about **justice** for the poor, but the wicked have no such concern. 1907

Truth

16:13 Kings take pleasure in honest lips; they value a man who speaks the **truth**. 3838

TRUTH AND THE WICKED

Justice

17:23 A wicked man accepts a bribe in secret to pervert the course of **justice**. 5477

18:5 It is not good to be partial to the wicked or to deprive the innocent of **justice**. 5477

19:28 A corrupt witness mocks at **justice**, and the mouth of the wicked gulps down evil. 5477

28:5 Evil men do not understand **justice**, but those who seek the LORD understand it fully. 5477

Right

21:7 The violence of the wicked will drag them away, for they refuse to do what is **right**. 5477

TRUTH AND THE TONGUE

True

8:7 My mouth speaks what is **true**, for my lips detest wickedness. 622

22:20-21 Have I not written thirty sayings for you, sayings of counsel and knowledge, [21] teaching you **true** and reliable words, so that you can give sound answers to him who sent you? 7999

Truthful

12:17 A **truthful** witness gives honest testimony, but a false witness tells lies. 575

12:19 **Truthful** lips endure forever, but a lying tongue lasts only a moment. 622

12:22 The LORD detests lying lips, but he delights in men who are **truthful**. 575

14:25 A **truthful** witness saves lives, but a false witness is deceitful. 622

TRUTH AND DEPENDABILITY

Faithfulness

3:3 Let love and **faithfulness** never leave you; bind them around your neck, write them on the tablet of your heart. 622

14:22 Do not those who plot evil go astray? But those who plan what is good find love and **faithfulness**. 622

16:6 Through love and **faithfulness** sin is atoned for; through the fear of the LORD a man avoids evil. 622

WAYS OF LIFE

Life portrayed as a journey is common to wisdom literature throughout the world, and Proverbs is no exception. But this wise teacher in Proverbs is the only one who can give us the right directions. Only God knows what the next step into our personal future will bring, but He wants us to be certain we are on the right path, headed for the right destination. Fools choose a crooked, thorny path characterized by injustice, immorality, lawlessness, duplicity, and violence. The scenery may be a dreamlike fantasy of exhilarating excitement, yet the ride ends in darkness, alienation from God, and death. In contrast the wise choose a less traveled road characterized by justice, morality, obedience, honesty, and peace. Realistically the wise open themselves to the truth and in the end they arrive satisfied with life, love, and immortality. Each of us chooses the road he will travel. For those who choose the path of wickedness the self-deception could become permanent and fatal. "But small is the gate and narrow the road that leads to life, and only a few find it" (Matt. 7:14).

WAYS OF LIFE RELATED TO THE WICKED		REFERENCE NUMBERS
Astray		
5:22-23	The evil deeds of a wicked man ensnare him; the cords of his sin hold him fast. [23] He will die for lack of discipline, led **astray** by his own great folly.	8706
Chases		
12:11	He who works his land will have abundant food, but he who **chases** fantasies lacks judgment.	8103
Course		
17:23	A wicked man accepts a bribe in secret to pervert the **course** of justice.	784
Folly		
19:3	A man's own **folly** ruins his life, yet his heart rages against the LORD.	222
Forsake		
28:4	Those who **forsake** the law praise the wicked, but those who keep the law resist them.	6440
Overthrows		
13:6	Righteousness guards the man of integrity, but wickedness **overthrows** the sinner.	6156
Path		
10:9	The man of integrity walks securely, but he who takes crooked **paths** will be found out.	2006
16:29	A violent man entices his neighbor and leads him down a **path** that is not good.	2006
22:5	In the **paths** of the wicked lie thorns and snares, but he who guards his soul stays far from them.	2006
28:10	He who leads the upright along an evil **path** will fall into his own trap, but the blameless will receive a good inheritance.	2006
Strays		
21:16	A man who **strays** from the path of understanding comes to rest in the company of the dead.	9494
Way		
1:31	they will eat the fruit of their **ways** and be filled with the fruit of their schemes.	2006

4:19	But the **way** of the wicked is like deep darkness; they do not know what makes them stumble.	2006
10:29	The **way** of the LORD is a refuge for the righteous, but it is the ruin of those who do evil.	2006
11:5	The righteousness of the blameless makes a straight **way** for them, but the wicked are brought down by their own wickedness.	2006
12:26	A righteous man is cautious in friendship, but the **way** of the wicked leads them astray.	2006
13:15	Good understanding wins favor, but the **way** of the unfaithful is hard.	2006
14:2	He whose walk is upright fears the LORD, but he whose **ways** are devious despises him.	2006
14:12	There is a **way** that seems right to a man, but in the end it leads to death.	2006
14:14	The faithless will be fully repaid for their **ways**, and the good man rewarded for his.	2006
15:9	The LORD detests the **way** of the wicked but he loves those who pursue righteousness.	2006
16:25	There is a **way** that seems right to a man, but in the end it leads to death.	2006
28:18	He whose walk is blameless is kept safe, but he whose **ways** are perverse will suddenly fall.	2006

WAYS OF LIFE RELATED TO THE RIGHTEOUS

Cautious

12:26	A righteous man is **cautious** in friendship, but the way of the wicked leads them astray.	9365

Conduct

21:8	The way of the guilty is devious, but the **conduct** of the innocent is upright.	7189

Guards

13:6	Righteousness **guards** the man of integrity, but wickedness overthrows the sinner.	5915
19:16	He who obeys instructions **guards** his life, but he who is contemptuous of his ways will die.	9068
22:5	In the paths of the wicked lie thorns and snares, but he who **guards** his soul stays far from them.	9068

Path

2:8-9	for he guards the course of the just and protects the way of his faithful ones. [9] Then you will understand what is right and just and fair— every good **path**.	5047
4:18	The **path** of the righteous is like the first gleam of dawn, shining ever brighter till the full light of day.	784
12:28	In the way of righteousness there is life; along that **path** is immortality.	5986
15:19	The way of the sluggard is blocked with thorns, but the **path** of the upright is a highway.	784
15:24	The **path** of life leads upward for the wise to keep him from going down to the grave.	784

Pursue

15:9	The LORD detests the way of the wicked but he loves those who **pursue** righteousness.	8103

		REFERENCE NUMBERS
21:21	He who **pursues** righteousness and love finds life, prosperity and honor.	8103

Walk
10:9	The man of integrity **walks** securely, but he who takes crooked paths will be found out.	2143
14:2	He whose **walk** is upright fears the LORD, but he whose ways are devious despises him.	2143
28:6	Better a poor man whose **walk** is blameless than a rich man whose ways are perverse.	2143
28:18	He whose **walk** is blameless is kept safe, but he whose ways are perverse will suddenly fall.	2143

WAYS OF LIFE RELATED TO WORK

Affairs
31:27	She watches over the **affairs** of her household and does not eat the bread of idleness.	2142

Chases
12:11	He who works his land will have abundant food, but he who **chases** fantasies lacks judgment.	8103
28:19	He who works his land will have abundant food, but the one who **chases** fantasies will have his fill of poverty.	8103

Ways
6:6	Go to the ant, you sluggard; consider its **ways** and be wise!	2006

WAYS OF LIFE RELATED TO IMMORALITY

Path
2:16-19	It will save you also from the adulteress, from the wayward wife with her seductive words, [17] who has left the partner of her youth and ignored the covenant she made before God. [18] For her house leads down to death and her **paths** to the spirits of the dead. [19] None who go to her return or attain the **paths** of life.	5047/784
5:6-10	She gives no thought to the way of life; her **paths** are crooked, but she knows it not. [7] Now then, my sons, listen to me; do not turn aside from what I say. [8] Keep to a **path** far from her, do not go near the door of her house, [9] lest you give your best strength to others and your years to one who is cruel, [10] lest strangers feast on your wealth and your toil enrich another man's house.	5047/2006

Strength
31:3	do not spend your **strength** on women, your vigor on those who ruin kings.	2657

Way
7:24-27	Now then, my sons, listen to me; pay attention to what I say. [25] Do not let your heart turn to her **ways** or stray into her paths. [26] Many are the victims she has brought down; her slain are a mighty throng. [27] Her house is a highway to the grave, leading down to the chambers of death.	2006
30:20	"This is the **way** of an adulteress: She eats and wipes her mouth and says, 'I've done nothing wrong.' "	2006

WAYS OF LIFE RELATED TO DISCIPLINE		REFERENCE NUMBERS

Forsake

| 28:4 | Those who **forsake** the law praise the wicked, but those who keep the law resist them. | 6440 |

Path

| 15:10 | Stern discipline awaits him who leaves the **path**; he who hates correction will die. | 784 |

Way

6:23	For these commands are a lamp, this teaching is a light, and the corrections of discipline are the **way** to life,	2006
10:17	He who heeds discipline shows the **way** to life, but whoever ignores correction leads others astray.	784
22:6	Train a child in the **way** he should go, and when he is old he will not turn from it.	2006 + 6584 + 7023

WAYS OF LIFE RELATED TO INSTRUCTION

Path

4:10-11	Listen, my son, accept what I say, and the years of your life will be many. [11] I guide you in the way of wisdom and lead you along straight **paths**.	5047
4:14-17	Do not set foot on the **path** of the wicked or walk in the way of evil men. [15] Avoid it, do not travel on it; turn from it and go on your way. [16] For they cannot sleep till they do evil; they are robbed of slumber till they make someone fall. [17] They eat the bread of wickedness and drink the wine of violence.	784
4:26	Make level **paths** for your feet and take only ways that are firm.	5047
23:19	Listen, my son, and be wise, and keep your heart on the right **path**.	2006

Way

2:12-15	Wisdom will save you from the **ways** of wicked men, from men whose words are perverse, [13] who leave the straight paths to walk in dark **ways**, [14] who delight in doing wrong and rejoice in the perverseness of evil, [15] whose paths are crooked and who are devious in their **ways**.	2006/2006/ 5047
2:20	Thus you will walk in the **ways** of good men and keep to the paths of the righteous.	2006
3:23	Then you will go on your **way** in safety, and your foot will not stumble;	2006
3:31	Do not envy a violent man or choose any of his **ways**,	2006
8:32	"Now then, my sons, listen to me; blessed are those who keep my **ways**."	2006
9:6	Leave your simple **ways** and you will live; walk in the **way** of understanding.	7344/2006
22:24-25	Do not make friends with a hot-tempered man, do not associate with one easily angered, [25] or you may learn his **ways** and get yourself ensnared.	784
23:26	My son, give me your heart and let your eyes keep to my **ways**,	2006

WAYS OF LIFE RELATED TO GOD

Course

| 16:9 | In his heart a man plans his **course**, but the LORD determines his steps. | 2006 |

REFERENCE
NUMBERS

Path

3:5-6   Trust in the Lord with all your heart and lean not on your own   784
         understanding; [6] in all your ways acknowledge him, and he
         will make your **paths** straight.

3:17   Her ways are pleasant ways, and all her **paths** are peace.   5986

8:1-2   Does not wisdom call out? Does not understanding raise her   5986
         voice? [2] On the heights along the way, where the **paths** meet,
         she takes her stand;

8:20   I walk in the way of righteousness, along the **paths** of justice,   5986

Way

5:21   For a man's **ways** are in full view of the Lord, and he exam-   2006
         ines all his paths.

10:29   The **way** of the Lord is a refuge for the righteous, but it is the   2006
         ruin of those who do evil.

16:2   All a man's **ways** seem innocent to him, but motives are   2006
         weighed by the Lord.

16:7   When a man's **ways** are pleasing to the Lord, he makes even   2006
         his enemies live at peace with him.

20:24   A man's steps are directed by the Lord. How then can anyone   2006
         understand his own **way**?

21:2   All a man's **ways** seem right to him, but the Lord weighs the   2006
         heart.

WICKEDNESS

The antithesis of righteousness, *wickedness*, is one of Proverb's dominant themes. Unfaithful in sexual relationships, untruthful in court, crooked in business, and contentious in the family—the wicked insanely wage war against their Maker. They huddle together and arrogantly plot their malicious schemes. Inflicting pain actually titillates their evil minds. Sometimes they seize control of entire nations, yet their duplicity and contentiousness can never build a country. Rebellion, anarchy, assassinations—these are the effects when sin rules. God assures us that not even the wicked can escape the boundaries of His sovereign plan. Thus the wise, discerning evil's characteristics, cry out for Christ to cleanse sinners from this self-deceptive foolishness. All of us are infected by this insidious plague. If we are honest we will face the truth and confess our wickedness to the Son of God. "And pray that we might be delivered from wicked and evil men, for not everyone has faith. But the Lord is faithful, and he will strengthen and protect you from the evil one" (2 Thess. 3:2-3).

WICKEDNESS AND IMMORALITY		REFERENCE NUMBERS
Unfaithful		
23:28	Like a bandit she lies in wait, and multiplies the **unfaithful** among men.	953
Wrath		
22:14	The mouth of an adulteress is a deep pit; he who is under the Lord's **wrath** will fall into it.	2404
Wrong		
30:20	"This is the way of an adulteress: She eats and wipes her mouth and says, 'I've done nothing **wrong.'"**	224

WICKEDNESS AND LYING		
Curse		
24:24	Whoever says to the guilty, "You are innocent"—peoples will **curse** him and nations denounce him.	7686
Detests		
12:22	The LORD **detests** lying lips, but he delights in men who are truthful.	9359
Evil		
12:20	There is deceit in the hearts of those who plot **evil**, but joy for those who promote peace.	8273
Wicked		
11:18	The **wicked** man earns deceptive wages, but he who sows righteousness reaps a sure reward.	8401
12:5	The plans of the righteous are just, but the advice of the **wicked** is deceitful.	8401
17:4	A **wicked** man listens to evil lips; a liar pays attention to a malicious tongue.	8317
Wickedness		
26:24-26	A malicious man disguises himself with his lips, but in his heart he harbors deceit. [25] Though his speech is charming, do not believe him, for seven abominations fill his heart. [26] His malice may be concealed by deception, but his **wickedness** will be exposed in the assembly.	8288

WICKEDNESS AND THE WICKED

Crafty

12:2   A good man obtains favor from the LORD, but the LORD condemns a **crafty** man.   4659

Crooked

10:9   The man of integrity walks securely, but he who takes **crooked** paths will be found out.   6835

Devious

14:2   He whose walk is upright fears the LORD, but he whose ways are **devious** despises him.   4279

Evil

2:12-15   Wisdom will save you from the ways of wicked men, from men whose words are perverse, [13] who leave the straight paths to walk in dark ways, [14] who delight in doing wrong and rejoice in the perverseness of **evil**, [15] whose paths are crooked and who are devious in their ways.   8273

6:14   who plots **evil** with deceit in his heart—he always stirs up dissension.   8273

6:16-19   There are six things the LORD hates, seven that are detestable to him: [17] haughty eyes, a lying tongue, hands that shed innocent blood, [18] a heart that devises wicked schemes, feet that are quick to rush into **evil**, [19] a false witness who pours out lies and a man who stirs up dissension among brothers.   8288

10:29   The way of the LORD is a refuge for the righteous, but it is the ruin of those who do **evil**.   224

11:19   The truly righteous man attains life, but he who pursues **evil** goes to his death.   8288

11:27   He who seeks good finds goodwill, but **evil** comes to him who searches for it.   8288

12:12   The wicked desire the plunder of **evil** men, but the root of the righteous flourishes.   8273

14:19   **Evil** men will bow down in the presence of the good, and the wicked at the gates of the righteous.   8273

14:22   Do not those who plot **evil** go astray? But those who plan what is good find love and faithfulness.   8273

17:11   An **evil** man is bent only on rebellion; a merciless official will be sent against him.   8273

17:13   If a man pays back **evil** for good, **evil** will never leave his house.   8288/8288

21:10   The wicked man craves **evil**; his neighbor gets no mercy from him.   8273

24:8   He who plots **evil** will be known as a schemer.   8317

24:19-20   Do not fret because of **evil** men or be envious of the wicked, [20] for the **evil** man has no future hope, and the lamp of the wicked will be snuffed out.   8317/8273

28:10   He who leads the upright along an **evil** path will fall into his own trap, but the blameless will receive a good inheritance.   8273

29:6   An **evil** man is snared by his own sin, but a righteous one can sing and be glad.   8273

Evildoers

21:15   When justice is done, it brings joy to the righteous but terror to **evildoers.**   224 + 7188

Harms

8:36   But whoever fails to find me **harms** himself; all who hate me love death."   2803

Perverse

3:31-32   Do not envy a violent man or choose any of his ways, [32] for   4279
the LORD detests a **perverse** man but takes the upright into his
confidence.

11:20   The LORD detests men of **perverse** heart but he delights in   6836
those whose ways are blameless.

16:28   A **perverse** man stirs up dissension, and a gossip separates   9337
close friends.

17:20   A man of **perverse** heart does not prosper; he whose tongue is   6836
deceitful falls into trouble.

28:6   Better a poor man whose walk is blameless than a rich man   6836
whose ways are **perverse.**

28:18   He whose walk is blameless is kept safe, but he whose ways are   6835
perverse will suddenly fall.

Sin

1:16   for their feet rush into **sin**, they are swift to shed blood.   8273

17:19   He who loves a quarrel loves **sin**; he who builds a high gate in-   7322
vites destruction.

21:4   Haughty eyes and a proud heart, the lamp of the wicked, are   2633
sin!

29:16   When the wicked thrive, so does **sin**, but the righteous will see   7322
their downfall.

Sinner

11:31   If the righteous receive their due on earth, how much more the   2627
ungodly and the **sinner**!

13:6   Righteousness guards the man of integrity, but wickedness   2633
overthrows the **sinner**.

13:21   Misfortune pursues the **sinner**, but prosperity is the reward of   2629
the righteous.

Trouble

28:14   Blessed is the man who always fears the LORD, but he who har-   8288
dens his heart falls into **trouble**.

Unfaithful

11:3   The integrity of the upright guides them, but the **unfaithful** are   953
destroyed by their duplicity.

11:6   The righteousness of the upright delivers them, but the **un-**   953
faithful are trapped by evil desires.

13:15   Good understanding wins favor, but the way of the **unfaithful**   953
is hard.

21:18   The wicked become a ransom for the righteous, and the **un-**   953
faithful for the upright.

Warped

12:8   A man is praised according to his wisdom, but men with   6390
warped minds are despised.

Wicked

2:21-22   For the upright will live in the land, and the blameless will re-   8401
main in it; [22] but the **wicked** will be cut off from the land,
and the unfaithful will be torn from it.

3:33   The Lord's curse is on the house of the **wicked**, but he blesses   8401
the home of the righteous.

4:19   But the way of the **wicked** is like deep darkness; they do not   8401
know what makes them stumble.

5:22   The evil deeds of a **wicked** man ensnare him; the cords of his   8401
sin hold him fast.

		REFERENCE NUMBERS
10:7	The memory of the righteous will be a blessing, but the name of the **wicked** will rot.	8401
10:16	The wages of the righteous bring them life, but the income of the **wicked** brings them punishment.	8401
10:24-25	What the **wicked** dreads will overtake him; what the righteous desire will be granted. [25] When the storm has swept by, the **wicked** are gone, but the righteous stand firm forever.	8401/8401
10:27-28	The fear of the LORD adds length to life, but the years of the **wicked** are cut short. [28] The prospect of the righteous is joy, but the hopes of the **wicked** come to nothing.	8401/8401
10:30	The righteous will never be uprooted, but the **wicked** will not remain in the land.	8401
11:5	The righteousness of the blameless makes a straight way for them, but the **wicked** are brought down by their own wickedness.	8401
11:7-8	When a **wicked** man dies, his hope perishes; all he expected from his power comes to nothing. [8] The righteous man is rescued from trouble, and it comes on the **wicked** instead.	8401
11:21	Be sure of this: The **wicked** will not go unpunished, but those who are righteous will go free.	8273
12:7	**wicked** men are overthrown and are no more, but the house of the righteous stands firm.	8401
12:10	A righteous man cares for the needs of his animal, but the kindest acts of the **wicked** are cruel.	8401
12:21	No harm befalls the righteous, but the **wicked** have their fill of trouble.	8401
12:26	A righteous man is cautious in friendship, but the way of the **wicked** leads them astray.	8401
13:17	A **wicked** messenger falls into trouble, but a trustworthy envoy brings healing.	8401
15:8-9	The LORD detests the sacrifice of the **wicked**, but the prayer of the upright pleases him. [9] The LORD detests the way of the **wicked** but he loves those who pursue righteousness.	8401
16:4	The LORD works out everything for his own ends—even the **wicked** for a day of disaster.	8401
21:7	The violence of the **wicked** will drag them away, for they refuse to do what is right.	8401
21:12	The Righteous One takes note of the house of the **wicked** and brings the **wicked** to ruin.	8401/8401
21:27	The sacrifice of the **wicked** is detestable—how much more so when brought with evil intent!	8401
21:29	A **wicked** man puts up a bold front, but an upright man gives thought to his ways.	8401
22:5	In the paths of the **wicked** lie thorns and snares, but he who guards his soul stays far from them.	6836
24:1-2	Do not envy **wicked** men, do not desire their company; [2] for their hearts plot violence, and their lips talk about making trouble.	8288
24:16	for though a righteous man falls seven times, he rises again, but the **wicked** are brought down by calamity.	8401
28:1	The **wicked** man flees though no one pursues, but the righteous are as bold as a lion.	8401
28:12	When the righteous triumph, there is great elation; but when the **wicked** rise to power, men go into hiding.	8401

28:28	When the **wicked** rise to power, people go into hiding; but when the **wicked** perish, the righteous thrive.	8401/4392ˢ
29:7	The righteous care about justice for the poor, but the **wicked** have no such concern.	8401
29:27	The righteous detest the dishonest; the **wicked** detest the upright.	8401

Wickedness

4:15-17	Avoid it, do not travel on it; turn from it and go on your way. [16] For they cannot sleep till they do evil; they are robbed of slumber till they make someone fall. [17] They eat the bread of **wickedness** and drink the wine of violence.	8400
12:3	A man cannot be established through **wickedness**, but the righteous cannot be uprooted.	8400
18:3	When **wickedness** comes, so does contempt, and with shame comes disgrace.	8401
22:8	He who sows **wickedness** reaps trouble, and the rod of his fury will be destroyed.	6406

Wretched

15:15	All the days of the oppressed are **wretched**, but the cheerful heart has a continual feast.	8273

Wrong

28:21	To show partiality is not good—yet a man will do **wrong** for a piece of bread.	7321
28:24	He who robs his father or mother and says, "It's not **wrong**"—he is partner to him who destroys.	7322

WICKEDNESS AND THE TONGUE

Deceit

26:24-25	A malicious man disguises himself with his lips, but in his heart he harbors **deceit**. [25] Though his speech is charming, do not believe him, for seven abominations fill his heart.	5327

Deceitful

15:4	The tongue that brings healing is a tree of life, but a **deceitful** tongue crushes the spirit.	6157

Evil

12:13	An **evil** man is trapped by his sinful talk, but a righteous man escapes trouble.	8273
15:28	The heart of the righteous weighs its answers, but the mouth of the wicked gushes **evil**.	8288
16:27	A scoundrel plots **evil**, and his speech is like a scorching fire.	8288
16:30	He who winks with his eye is plotting perversity; he who purses his lips is bent on **evil**.	8288
26:23	Like a coating of glaze over earthenware are fervent lips with an **evil** heart.	8273

Perverse

16:28	A **perverse** man stirs up dissension, and a gossip separates close friends.	9337
17:20	A man of **perverse** heart does not prosper; he whose tongue is deceitful falls into trouble.	6836

Sin

10:19	When words are many, **sin** is not absent, but he who holds his tongue is wise.	7322

Unfaithful

13:2   From the fruit of his lips a man enjoys good things, but the **un-**   953
faithful have a craving for violence.

22:12   The eyes of the LORD keep watch over knowledge, but he frus-   953
trates the words of the **unfaithful**.

Wicked

10:6   Blessings crown the head of the righteous, but violence over-   8401
whelms the mouth of the **wicked**.

10:11   The mouth of the righteous is a fountain of life, but violence   8401
overwhelms the mouth of the **wicked**.

10:20   The tongue of the righteous is choice silver, but the heart of the   8401
wicked is of little value.

10:32   The lips of the righteous know what is fitting, but the mouth of   8401
the **wicked** only what is perverse.

11:11   Through the blessing of the upright a city is exalted, but by the   8401
mouth of the **wicked** it is destroyed.

12:6   The words of the **wicked** lie in wait for blood, but the speech of   8401
the upright rescues them.

19:28   A corrupt witness mocks at justice, and the mouth of the **wick-**   8401
ed gulps down evil.

24:1-2   Do not envy **wicked** men, do not desire their company; [2] for   8288
their hearts plot violence, and their lips talk about making trouble.

WICKEDNESS AND THE FOOL

Evil

10:23   A fool finds pleasure in **evil** conduct, but a man of understand-   2365
ing delights in wisdom.

13:19   A longing fulfilled is sweet to the soul, but fools detest turning   8273
from **evil**.

Folly

19:3   A man's own **folly** ruins his life, yet his heart rages against the   222
LORD.

Perverse

19:1   Better a poor man whose walk is blameless than a fool whose   6836
lips are **perverse**.

Reckless

14:16   A wise man fears the LORD and shuns evil, but a fool is hot-   1053
headed and **reckless**.

Sin

14:9   Fools mock at making amends for **sin**, but goodwill is found   871
among the upright.

24:9   The schemes of folly are **sin**, and men detest a mocker.   2633

Strife

18:6   A fool's lips bring him **strife**, and his mouth invites a beating.   8190

22:10   Drive out the mocker, and out goes **strife**; quarrels and insults   4506
are ended.

Suffer

22:3   A prudent man sees danger and takes refuge, but the simple   6740
keep going and **suffer** for it.

27:12   The prudent see danger and take refuge, but the simple keep   6740
going and **suffer** for it.

WICKEDNESS AND PRIDE

Detests
16:5   The LORD **detests** all the proud of heart. Be sure of this: They will not go unpunished.   9359

Quarrels
13:10   Pride only breeds **quarrels**, but wisdom is found in those who take advice.   5175

Sin
21:4   Haughty eyes and a proud heart, the lamp of the wicked, are **sin**!   2633

WICKEDNESS AND AUTHORITIES

Detest
16:12   Kings **detest** wrongdoing, for a throne is established through righteousness.   9359

Evil
20:8   When a king sits on his throne to judge, he winnows out all **evil** with his eyes.   8273

Justice
16:10   The lips of a king speak as an oracle, and his mouth should not betray **justice**.   5477

Rebellious
28:2   When a country is **rebellious**, it has many rulers, but a man of understanding and knowledge maintains order.   7322

Wicked
20:26   A wise king winnows out the **wicked**; he drives the threshing wheel over them.   8401

25:4-5   Remove the dross from the silver, and out comes material for the silversmith; [5] remove the **wicked** from the king's presence, and his throne will be established through righteousness.   8401

28:12   When the righteous triumph, there is great elation; but when the **wicked** rise to power, men go into hiding.   8401

28:15   Like a roaring lion or a charging bear is a **wicked** man ruling over a helpless people.   8401

29:2   When the righteous thrive, the people rejoice; when the **wicked** rule, the people groan.   8401

29:12   If a ruler listens to lies, all his officials become **wicked**.   8401

WICKEDNESS AND JUDGMENT

Corrupt
19:28   A **corrupt** witness mocks at justice, and the mouth of the wicked gulps down evil.   1175

Detests
17:15   Acquitting the guilty and condemning the innocent—the LORD **detests** them both.   9359

Evil
20:8   When a king sits on his throne to judge, he winnows out all **evil** with his eyes.   8273

28:5   **Evil** men do not understand justice, but those who seek the LORD understand it fully.   8273

Pervert
17:23   A wicked man accepts a bribe in secret to **pervert** the course of justice.   5742

Wicked

18:5   It is not good to be partial to the **wicked** or to deprive the inno-   8401
cent of justice.

21:7   The violence of the **wicked** will drag them away, for they re-   8401
fuse to do what is right.

Wrath

11:23   The desire of the righteous ends only in good, but the hope of   6301
the wicked only in **wrath**.

WICKEDNESS AND THE LAW

Detestable

28:9   If anyone turns a deaf ear to the law, even his prayers are **detes-**   9359
table.

Wicked

28:4   Those who forsake the law praise the **wicked**, but those who   8401
keep the law resist them.

WICKEDNESS AND ANGER

Dissension

29:22   An angry man stirs up **dissension**, and a hot-tempered one   4506
commits many sins.

Evil

26:23   Like a coating of glaze over earthenware are fervent lips with   8273
an **evil** heart.

Fury

22:8   He who sows wickedness reaps trouble, and the rod of his **fury**   6301
will be destroyed.

Hatred

10:12   **Hatred** stirs up dissension, but love covers over all wrongs.   8534

WICKEDNESS AND CONTENTIONS

Disputes

18:18-19 Casting the lot settles **disputes** and keeps strong opponents   4506/4506
apart. [19] An offended brother is more unyielding than a forti-
fied city, and **disputes** are like the barred gates of a citadel.

Quarrel

17:14   Starting a **quarrel** is like breaching a dam; so drop the matter   4506
before a dispute breaks out.

Quarrels

22:10   Drive out the mocker, and out goes strife; **quarrels** and insults   1907
are ended.

Quarrelsome

26:21   As charcoal to embers and as wood to fire, so is a **quarrelsome**   4506
man for kindling strife.

CONTRASTS TO WICKEDNESS

Our society often sees "gray" when it comes to moral issues. Proverbs exposes this unethical color blindness as naivete and as a failure to discipline ourselves to learn to make clean moral decisions. Mental keenness concerning right and wrong is developed by carefully observing the many contrasts between the character traits and life destinies of the righteous and the wicked. "But solid food is for the mature, who by constant use have trained themselves to distinguish good from evil" (Heb. 5:14).

WICKEDNESS CONTRASTED TO THE RIGHTEOUS		REFERENCE NUMBERS
Blameless		
11:5	The righteousness of the **blameless** makes a straight way for them, but the wicked are brought down by their own wickedness.	9459
28:10	He who leads the upright along an evil path will fall into his own trap, but the **blameless** will receive a good inheritance.	9459
28:18	He whose walk is **blameless** is kept safe, but he whose ways are perverse will suddenly fall.	9459
Good		
11:27	He who seeks **good** finds goodwill, but evil comes to him who searches for it.	3202
13:22	A **good** man leaves an inheritance for his children's children, but a sinner's wealth is stored up for the righteous.	3202
14:22	Do not those who plot evil go astray? But those who plan what is **good** find love and faithfulness.	3202
Integrity		
10:9	The man of **integrity** walks securely, but he who takes crooked paths will be found out.	9448
Prudent		
22:3	A **prudent** man sees danger and takes refuge, but the simple keep going and suffer for it.	6874
27:12	The **prudent** see danger and take refuge, but the simple keep going and suffer for it.	6874
Righteous		
3:33	The Lord's curse is on the house of the wicked, but he blesses the home of the **righteous**.	7404
4:18	The path of the **righteous** is like the first gleam of dawn, shining ever brighter till the full light of day.	7404
10:3	The Lord does not let the **righteous** go hungry but he thwarts the craving of the wicked.	7404
10:6-7	Blessings crown the head of the **righteous**, but violence overwhelms the mouth of the wicked. [7] The memory of the **righteous** will be a blessing, but the name of the wicked will rot.	7404/7404
10:16	The wages of the **righteous** bring them life, but the income of the wicked brings them punishment.	7404
10:24-25	What the wicked dreads will overtake him; what the **righteous** desire will be granted. [25] When the storm has swept by, the wicked are gone, but the **righteous** stand firm forever.	7404/7404
10:28	The prospect of the **righteous** is joy, but the hopes of the wicked come to nothing.	7404

		REFERENCE NUMBERS
10:30	The **righteous** will never be uprooted, but the wicked will not remain in the land.	7404
11:8-10	The **righteous** man is rescued from trouble, and it comes on the wicked instead. [9] With his mouth the godless destroys his neighbor, but through knowledge the **righteous** escape. [10] When the **righteous** prosper, the city rejoices; when the wicked perish, there are shouts of joy.	7404/7404/ 7404
11:19	The truly **righteous** man attains life, but he who pursues evil goes to his death.	7407
11:21	Be sure of this: The wicked will not go unpunished, but those who are **righteous** will go free.	2446 + 7404
11:23	The desire of the **righteous** ends only in good, but the hope of the wicked only in wrath.	7404
11:31	If the **righteous** receive their due on earth, how much more the ungodly and the sinner!	7404
12:3	A man cannot be established through wickedness, but the **righteous** cannot be uprooted.	7404
12:5	The plans of the **righteous** are just, but the advice of the wicked is deceitful.	7404
12:7	Wicked men are overthrown and are no more, but the house of the **righteous** stands firm.	7404
12:10	A **righteous** man cares for the needs of his animal, but the kindest acts of the wicked are cruel.	7404
12:12-13	The wicked desire the plunder of evil men, but the root of the **righteous** flourishes. [13] An evil man is trapped by his sinful talk, but a **righteous** man escapes trouble.	7404/7404
12:21	No harm befalls the **righteous**, but the wicked have their fill of trouble.	7404
12:26	A **righteous** man is cautious in friendship, but the way of the wicked leads them astray.	7404
13:21	Misfortune pursues the sinner, but prosperity is the reward of the **righteous**.	7404
14:19	Evil men will bow down in the presence of the good, and the wicked at the gates of the **righteous**.	7404
15:28	The heart of the **righteous** weighs its answers, but the mouth of the wicked gushes evil.	7404
24:15-16	Do not lie in wait like an outlaw against a **righteous** man's house, do not raid his dwelling place; [16] for though a **righteous** man falls seven times, he rises again, but the wicked are brought down by calamity.	7404/7404
28:1	The wicked man flees though no one pursues, but the **righteous** are as bold as a lion.	7404
28:12	When the **righteous** triumph, there is great elation; but when the wicked rise to power, men go into hiding.	7404
28:28	When the wicked rise to power, people go into hiding; but when the wicked perish, the **righteous** thrive.	7404
29:6-7	An evil man is snared by his own sin, but a **righteous** one can sing and be glad. [7] The **righteous** care about justice for the poor, but the wicked have no such concern.	7404/7404

Righteousness

10:2	Ill-gotten treasures are of no value, but **righteousness** delivers from death.	7407
11:18	The wicked man earns deceptive wages, but he who sows **righteousness** reaps a sure reward.	7407

		REFERENCE NUMBERS
13:6	**Righteousness** guards the man of integrity, but wickedness overthrows the sinner.	7407
14:34	**Righteousness** exalts a nation, but sin is a disgrace to any people.	7407
25:5	remove the wicked from the king's presence, and his throne will be established through **righteousness**.	7406

Trustworthy

13:17	A wicked messenger falls into trouble, but a **trustworthy** envoy brings healing.	574

Upright

3:31-32	Do not envy a violent man or choose any of his ways, [32] for the LORD detests a perverse man but takes the **upright** into his confidence.	3838
11:3	The integrity of the **upright** guides them, but the unfaithful are destroyed by their duplicity.	3838
11:6	The righteousness of the **upright** delivers them, but the unfaithful are trapped by evil desires.	3838
11:11	Through the blessing of the **upright** a city is exalted, but by the mouth of the wicked it is destroyed.	3838
14:9	Fools mock at making amends for sin, but goodwill is found among the **upright.**	3838
15:8	The LORD detests the sacrifice of the wicked, but the prayer of the **upright** pleases him.	3838
16:17	The highway of the **upright** avoids evil; he who guards his way guards his life.	3838
21:18	The wicked become a ransom for the righteous, and the unfaithful for the **upright**.	3838
21:29	A wicked man puts up a bold front, but an **upright** man gives thought to his ways.	3838

WICKEDNESS CONTRASTED TO THE TONGUE

Good

13:2	From the fruit of his lips a man enjoys **good** things, but the unfaithful have a craving for violence.	3202

Healing

15:4	The tongue that brings **healing** is a tree of life, but a deceitful tongue crushes the spirit.	5340

Righteous

10:11	The mouth of the **righteous** is a fountain of life, but violence overwhelms the mouth of the wicked.	7404
10:20	The tongue of the **righteous** is choice silver, but the heart of the wicked is of little value.	7404
10:32	The lips of the **righteous** know what is fitting, but the mouth of the wicked only what is perverse.	7404

Upright

12:6	The words of the wicked lie in wait for blood, but the speech of the **upright** rescues them.	3838

WICKEDNESS CONTRASTED TO THE FEAR OF THE LORD

Fear/Lord

3:7	Do not be wise in your own eyes; **fear the LORD** and shun evil.	3707/3378

8:13	To **fear the Lord** is to hate evil; I hate pride and arrogance, evil behavior and perverse speech.	3711/3378
10:27	The **fear of the Lord** adds length to life, but the years of the wicked are cut short.	3711/3378
14:2	He whose walk is upright **fears the Lord,** but he whose ways are devious despises him.	3707/3378
16:6	Through love and faithfulness sin is atoned for; through the **fear of the Lord** a man avoids evil.	3711/3378
19:23	The **fear of the Lord** leads to life: Then one rests content, untouched by trouble.	3711/3378
23:17	Do not let your heart envy sinners, but always be zealous for the **fear of the Lord**.	3711/3378
28:14	Blessed is the man who always **fears the Lord**, but he who hardens his heart falls into trouble.	7064/NIH

Lord

10:29	The way of the **Lord** is a refuge for the righteous, but it is the ruin of those who do evil.	3378
12:2	A good man obtains favor from the **Lord**, but the **Lord** condemns a crafty man.	3378/NIH
15:3	The eyes of the **Lord** are everywhere, keeping watch on the wicked and the good.	3378
20:22	Do not say, "I'll pay you back for this wrong!" Wait for the **Lord**, and he will deliver you.	3378
22:12	The eyes of the **Lord** keep watch over knowledge, but he frustrates the words of the unfaithful.	3378
28:5	Evil men do not understand justice, but those who seek the **Lord** understand it fully.	3378

WICKEDNESS CONTRASTED TO WISDOM

Understanding

13:15	Good **understanding** wins favor, but the way of the unfaithful is hard.	8507
28:2	When a country is rebellious, it has many rulers, but a man of **understanding** and knowledge maintains order.	1067

Wisdom

10:23	A fool finds pleasure in evil conduct, but a man of understanding delights in **wisdom**.	2683
10:31	The mouth of the righteous brings forth **wisdom**, but a perverse tongue will be cut out.	2683
12:8	A man is praised according to his **wisdom**, but men with warped minds are despised.	8507

Wise

10:19	When words are many, sin is not absent, but he who holds his tongue is **wise**.	8505
14:16	A **wise** man fears the Lord and shuns evil, but a fool is hotheaded and reckless.	2682

WICKEDNESS CONTRASTED TO DISCIPLINE

Beatings

20:30	Blows and wounds cleanse away evil, and **beatings** purge the inmost being.	4804

WISDOM

The theme of Proverbs is "to internalize the art of skillful living which comes through disciplined training; to discern the words of insight" (1:2, Wyrtzen paraphrase). Proverbial wisdom is practical, skillful living—the application of God's life blueprint in everything from the way we talk to the way we worship. More priceless than gold and rubies, this blueprint can deliver the gift of life, and is freely available to all who will open their ears to God's teaching. A relationship of reverence, trust, and intimacy with God is the first step in wise conduct. Let's listen attentively as God teaches us the facts of life.

WISDOM AND INSTRUCTION		REFERENCE NUMBERS
Judgment		
3:21-22	My son, preserve sound **judgment** and discernment, do not let them out of your sight; [22] they will be life for you, an ornament to grace your neck.	9370
Knowledge		
2:10	For wisdom will enter your heart, and **knowledge** will be pleasant to your soul.	1981
8:10	Choose my instruction instead of silver, **knowledge** rather than choice gold,	1981
12:1	Whoever loves discipline loves **knowledge**, but he who hates correction is stupid.	1981
14:7	Stay away from a foolish man, for you will not find **knowledge** on his lips.	1981
19:27	Stop listening to instruction, my son, and you will stray from the words of **knowledge**.	1981
21:11	When a mocker is punished, the simple gain wisdom; when a wise man is instructed, he gets **knowledge**.	1981
22:20-21	Have I not written thirty sayings for you, sayings of counsel and **knowledge**, [21] teaching you true and reliable words, so that you can give sound answers to him who sent you?	1981
23:12	Apply your heart to instruction and your ears to words of **knowledge**.	1981
Teach		
22:17-18	Pay attention and listen to the sayings of the wise; apply your heart to what I **teach**, [18] for it is pleasing when you keep them in your heart and have all of them ready on your lips.	1981
Wisdom		
4:10-13	Listen, my son, accept what I say, and the years of your life will be many. [11] I guide you in the way of **wisdom** and lead you along straight paths. [12] When you walk, your steps will not be hampered; when you run, you will not stumble. [13] Hold on to instruction, do not let it go; guard it well, for it is your life.	2683
7:4	Say to **wisdom**, "You are my sister," and call understanding your kinsman;	2683
8:1	Does not **wisdom** call out? Does not understanding raise her voice?	2683
8:10-11	Choose my instruction instead of silver, knowledge rather than choice gold, [11] for **wisdom** is more precious than rubies, and nothing you desire can compare with her.	2683

9:1-6	**Wisdom** has built her house; she has hewn out its seven pillars. [2] She has prepared her meat and mixed her wine; she has also set her table. [3] She has sent out her maids, and she calls from the highest point of the city. [4] "Let all who are simple come in here!" she says to those who lack judgment. [5] "Come, eat my food and drink the wine I have mixed. [6] Leave your simple ways and you will live; walk in the way of understanding."	2684
12:8	A man is praised according to his **wisdom**, but men with warped minds are despised.	8507
13:10	Pride only breeds quarrels, but **wisdom** is found in those who take advice.	2683
19:8	He who gets **wisdom** loves his own soul; he who cherishes understanding prospers.	4213
23:4	Do not wear yourself out to get rich; have the **wisdom** to show restraint.	1069
23:9	Do not speak to a fool, for he will scorn the **wisdom** of your words.	8507
24:3	By **wisdom** a house is built, and through understanding it is established;	2683

Wise

3:7	Do not be **wise** in your own eyes; fear the LORD and shun evil.	2682
6:6	Go to the ant, you sluggard; consider its ways and be **wise**!	2681
8:33	Listen to my instruction and be **wise**; do not ignore it.	2681
9:8-9	Do not rebuke a mocker or he will hate you; rebuke a **wise** man and he will love you. [9] Instruct a **wise** man and he will be wiser still; teach a righteous man and he will add to his learning.	2682/2682
9:12	"If you are **wise**, your wisdom will reward you; if you are a mocker, you alone will suffer."	2681
10:8	The **wise** in heart accept commands, but a chattering fool comes to ruin.	2682
11:29	He who brings trouble on his family will inherit only wind, and the fool will be servant to the **wise**.	2682 + 4213
12:15	The way of a fool seems right to him, but a **wise** man listens to advice.	2682
13:14	The teaching of the **wise** is a fountain of life, turning a man from the snares of death.	2682
13:20	He who walks with the **wise** grows **wise**, but a companion of fools suffers harm.	2682/2681
15:24	The path of life leads upward for the **wise** to keep him from going down to the grave.	8505
19:20	Listen to advice and accept instruction, and in the end you will be **wise**.	2681
24:5-6	A **wise** man has great power, and a man of knowledge increases strength; [6] for waging war you need guidance, and for victory many advisers.	2682
24:23	These also are sayings of the **wise**: To show partiality in judging is not good:	2682
26:12	Do you see a man **wise** in his own eyes? There is more hope for a fool than for him.	2682
29:9	If a **wise** man goes to court with a fool, the fool rages and scoffs, and there is no peace.	2682

WISDOM AND THE RIGHTEOUS	REFERENCE NUMBERS

Knowledge

11:9   With his mouth the godless destroys his neighbor, but through **knowledge** the righteous escape.   1981

12:23   A prudent man keeps his **knowledge** to himself, but the heart of fools blurts out folly.   1981

Righteous

10:21   The lips of the **righteous** nourish many, but fools die for lack of judgment.   7404

Understanding

15:21   Folly delights a man who lacks judgment, but a man of **understanding** keeps a straight course.   9312

Wisdom

10:31   The mouth of the righteous brings forth **wisdom**, but a perverse tongue will be cut out.   2683

14:8   The **wisdom** of the prudent is to give thought to their ways, but the folly of fools is deception.   2683

Wise

11:30   The fruit of the righteous is a tree of life, and he who wins souls is **wise**.   2682

16:21   The **wise** in heart are called discerning, and pleasant words promote instruction.   2682

WISDOM AND THE TONGUE

Discerning

10:13   Wisdom is found on the lips of the **discerning**, but a rod is for the back of him who lacks judgment.   1067

Knowledge

5:1-2   My son, pay attention to my wisdom, listen well to my words of insight, [2] that you may maintain discretion and your lips may preserve **knowledge**.   1981

11:9   With his mouth the godless destroys his neighbor, but through **knowledge** the righteous escape.   1981

15:2   The tongue of the wise commends **knowledge**, but the mouth of the fool gushes folly.   1981

15:7   The lips of the wise spread **knowledge**; not so the hearts of fools.   1981

17:27   A man of **knowledge** uses words with restraint, and a man of understanding is even-tempered.   1981 + 3359

20:15   Gold there is, and rubies in abundance, but lips that speak **knowledge** are a rare jewel.   1981

Understanding

11:12   A man who lacks judgment derides his neighbor, but a man of **understanding** holds his tongue.   9312

17:27   A man of knowledge uses words with restraint, and a man of **understanding** is even-tempered.   9312

Wisdom

10:31-32   The mouth of the righteous brings forth **wisdom**, but a perverse tongue will be cut out. [32] The lips of the righteous know what is fitting, but the mouth of the wicked only what is perverse.   2683

18:4   The words of a man's mouth are deep waters, but the fountain of **wisdom** is a bubbling brook.   2683

23:9   Do not speak to a fool, for he will scorn the **wisdom** of your words.   8507

		REFERENCE NUMBERS
31:26	She speaks with **wisdom**, and faithful instruction is on her tongue.	2683

Wise

10:19	When words are many, sin is not absent, but he who holds his tongue is **wise**.	8505
12:18	Reckless words pierce like a sword, but the tongue of the **wise** brings healing.	2682
14:3	A fool's talk brings a rod to his back, but the lips of the **wise** protect them.	2682
16:21	The **wise** in heart are called discerning, and pleasant words promote instruction.	2682
16:23	A **wise** man's heart guides his mouth, and his lips promote instruction.	2682
26:5	Answer a fool according to his folly, or he will be **wise** in his own eyes.	2682

WISDOM AND THE LORD

Instruction

| 16:20 | Whoever gives heed to **instruction** prospers, and blessed is he who trusts in the LORD. | 1821 |

Knowledge

1:7	The fear of the LORD is the beginning of **knowledge**, but fools despise wisdom and discipline.	1981
2:1-6	My son, if you accept my words and store up my commands within you, [2] turning your ear to wisdom and applying your heart to understanding, [3] and if you call out for insight and cry aloud for understanding, [4] and if you look for it as for silver and search for it as for hidden treasure, [5] then you will understand the fear of the LORD and find the **knowledge** of God. [6] For the LORD gives wisdom, and from his mouth come **knowledge** and understanding.	1981/1981
8:12-13	"I, wisdom, dwell together with prudence; I possess **knowledge** and discretion. [13] To fear the LORD is to hate evil; I hate pride and arrogance, evil behavior and perverse speech."	1981
22:12	The eyes of the LORD keep watch over **knowledge**, but he frustrates the words of the unfaithful.	1981

Plan

| 21:30 | There is no wisdom, no insight, no **plan** that can succeed against the LORD. | 6783 |

Understanding

3:5	Trust in the LORD with all your heart and lean not on your own **understanding**;	1069
20:24	A man's steps are directed by the LORD. How then can anyone **understand** his own way?	1067
28:5	Evil men do not **understand** justice, but those who seek the LORD **understand** it fully.	1067/1067

Wisdom

1:20	**Wisdom** calls aloud in the street, she raises her voice in the public squares;	2684
9:10	"The fear of the LORD is the beginning of **wisdom**, and knowledge of the Holy One is understanding."	2683
15:33	The fear of the LORD teaches a man **wisdom**, and humility comes before honor.	2683

Wise
3:7   Do not be **wise** in your own eyes; fear the Lord and shun evil.   2682
14:16   A **wise** man fears the Lord and shuns evil, but a fool is hot-   2682
       headed and reckless.

WISDOM AND KNOWLEDGE

Knowledge
8:6-9   Listen, for I have worthy things to say; I open my lips to speak   1981
       what is right. [7] My mouth speaks what is true, for my lips
       detest wickedness. [8] All the words of my mouth are just;
       none of them is crooked or perverse. [9] To the discerning all
       of them are right; they are faultless to those who have **knowl-
edge**.
9:10   "The fear of the Lord is the beginning of wisdom, and **knowl-**   1981
       edge of the Holy One is understanding."
10:14   Wise men store up **knowledge**, but the mouth of a fool invites   1981
       ruin.
11:9   With his mouth the godless destroys his neighbor, but through   1981
       knowledge the righteous escape.
12:23   A prudent man keeps his **knowledge** to himself, but the heart   1981
       of fools blurts out folly.
13:16   Every prudent man acts out of **knowledge**, but a fool exposes   1981
       his folly.
14:6   The mocker seeks wisdom and finds none, but **knowledge**   1981
       comes easily to the discerning.
14:18   The simple inherit folly, but the prudent are crowned with   1981
       knowledge.
15:2   The tongue of the wise commends **knowledge**, but the mouth   1981
       of the fool gushes folly.
15:7   The lips of the wise spread **knowledge**; not so the hearts of   1981
       fools.
15:14   The discerning heart seeks **knowledge**, but the mouth of a fool   1981
       feeds on folly.
18:15   The heart of the discerning acquires **knowledge**; the ears of the   1981
       wise seek it out.
19:2   It is not good to have zeal without **knowledge**, nor to be hasty   1981
       and miss the way.
21:11   When a mocker is punished, the simple gain wisdom; when a   1981
       wise man is instructed, he gets **knowledge**.
24:3-5   By wisdom a house is built, and through understanding it is es-   1981/1981
       tablished; [4] through **knowledge** its rooms are filled with rare
       and beautiful treasures.
       [5] A wise man has great power, and a man of **knowledge**
       increases strength;
28:2   When a country is rebellious, it has many rulers, but a man of   3359
       understanding and **knowledge** maintains order.

WISDOM AND DISCIPLINE

Discernment
17:10   A rebuke impresses a man of **discernment** more than a hun-   1067
       dred lashes a fool.
Knowledge
19:25   Flog a mocker, and the simple will learn prudence; rebuke a   1981
       discerning man, and he will gain **knowledge**.

21:11   When a mocker is punished, the simple gain wisdom; when a   1981
wise man is instructed, he gets **knowledge**.

Understanding
15:32   He who ignores discipline despises himself, but whoever heeds   4213
correction gains **understanding**.

Wisdom
29:15   The rod of correction imparts **wisdom**, but a child left to him-   2683
self disgraces his mother.

Wise
9:8-9   Do not rebuke a mocker or he will hate you; rebuke a **wise** man   2682/2682
and he will love you. [9] Instruct a **wise** man and he will be
wiser still; teach a righteous man and he will add to his learning.

15:31   He who listens to a life-giving rebuke will be at home among   2682
the **wise**.

25:12   Like an earring of gold or an ornament of fine gold is a **wise**   2682
man's rebuke to a listening ear.

WISDOM AND BLESSINGS

Understanding
3:13   Blessed is the man who finds wisdom, the man who gains **un-**   9312
derstanding,

Wisdom
24:14   Know also that **wisdom** is sweet to your soul; if you find it,   2683
there is a future hope for you, and your hope will not be cut off.

Wise
3:35   The **wise** inherit honor, but fools he holds up to shame.   2682

21:20   In the house of the **wise** are stores of choice food and oil, but a   2682
foolish man devours all he has.

WISDOM AND AUTHORITIES

Knowledge
28:2   When a country is rebellious, it has many rulers, but a man of   3359
understanding and **knowledge** maintains order.

Wise
14:35   A king delights in a **wise** servant, but a shameful servant incurs   8505
his wrath.

16:14   A king's wrath is a messenger of death, but a **wise** man will   2682
appease it.

20:26   A **wise** king winnows out the wicked; he drives the threshing   2682
wheel over them.

WISDOM AND UNDERSTANDING

Discerning
10:13   Wisdom is found on the lips of the **discerning**, but a rod is for   1067
the back of him who lacks judgment.

14:6   The mocker seeks wisdom and finds none, but knowledge   1067
comes easily to the **discerning**.

14:33   Wisdom reposes in the heart of the **discerning** and even among   1067
fools she lets herself be known.

17:24   A **discerning** man keeps wisdom in view, but a fool's eyes   1067
wander to the ends of the earth.

Discernment

28:11   A rich man may be wise in his own eyes, but a poor man who   1067
has **discernment** sees through him.

Discretion

5:1-2   My son, pay attention to my wisdom, listen well to my words   4659
of insight, [2] that you may maintain **discretion** and your lips
may preserve knowledge.

Understanding

1:1-6   The proverbs of Solomon son of David, king of Israel: 1067/1067
[2] for attaining wisdom and discipline; for **understanding**
words of insight; [3] for acquiring a disciplined and prudent
life, doing what is right and just and fair; [4] for giving prudence to the simple, knowledge and discretion to the
young—[5] let the wise listen and add to their learning, and let
the discerning get guidance—[6] for **understanding** proverbs
and parables, the sayings and riddles of the wise.

2:1-5   My son, if you accept my words and store up my commands   9312/9312
within you, [2] turning your ear to wisdom and applying your
heart to **understanding**, [3] and if you call out for insight and
cry aloud for **understanding**, [4] and if you look for it as for
silver and search for it as for hidden treasure, [5] then you will
understand the fear of the LORD and find the knowledge of
God.

2:9-11   Then you will understand what is right and just and fair—every   9312
good path. [10] For wisdom will enter your heart, and knowl-
edge will be pleasant to your soul. [11] Discretion will protect
you, and **understanding** will guard you.

3:13   Blessed is the man who finds wisdom, the man who gains **un-**   9312
derstanding,

4:5-9   "Get wisdom, get **understanding**; do not forget my words or   1069/1069
swerve from them. [6] Do not forsake wisdom, and she will
protect you; love her, and she will watch over you. [7] Wisdom
is supreme; therefore get wisdom. Though it cost all you have,
get **understanding**. [8] Esteem her, and she will exalt you; embrace her, and she will honor you. [9] She will set a garland of
grace on your head and present you with a crown of splendor."

7:4-5   Say to wisdom, "You are my sister," and call **understanding**   1069
your kinsman; [5] they will keep you from the adulteress, from
the wayward wife with her seductive words.

8:1-5   Does not wisdom call out? Does not **understanding** raise her   9312/4213
voice? [2] On the heights along the way, where the paths meet,
she takes her stand; [3] beside the gates leading into the city, at
the entrances, she cries aloud: [4] "To you, O men, I call out; I
raise my voice to all mankind. [5] You who are simple, gain
prudence; you who are foolish, gain **understanding**."

8:14   Counsel and sound judgment are mine; I have **understanding**   1069
and power.

9:6   Leave your simple ways and you will live; walk in the way of   1069
understanding.

11:12   A man who lacks judgment derides his neighbor, but a man of   9312
understanding holds his tongue.

13:15   Good **understanding** wins favor, but the way of the unfaithful   8507
is hard.

15:32   He who ignores discipline despises himself, but whoever heeds   4213
correction gains **understanding**.

		REFERENCE NUMBERS
16:16	How much better to get wisdom than gold, to choose **understanding** rather than silver!	1069
16:22	**Understanding** is a fountain of life to those who have it, but folly brings punishment to fools.	8507
17:27	A man of knowledge uses words with restraint, and a man of **understanding** is even-tempered.	9312
19:8	He who gets wisdom loves his own soul; he who cherishes **understanding** prospers.	9312
20:5	The purposes of a man's heart are deep waters, but a man of **understanding** draws them out.	9312
21:16	A man who strays from the path of **understanding** comes to rest in the company of the dead.	8505
23:23	Buy the truth and do not sell it; get wisdom, discipline and **understanding**.	1069
24:3-4	By wisdom a house is built, and through **understanding** it is established; [4] through knowledge its rooms are filled with rare and beautiful treasures.	9312

WISDOM AND ANGER

Understanding

11:12	A man who lacks judgment derides his neighbor, but a man of **understanding** holds his tongue.	9312
14:29	A patient man has great **understanding**, but a quick-tempered man displays folly.	9312

Wise

29:8	Mockers stir up a city, but **wise** men turn away anger.	2682
29:11	A fool gives full vent to his anger, but a **wise** man keeps himself under control.	2682

WISDOM AND THE WISE

Judgment

18:1	An unfriendly man pursues selfish ends; he defies all sound **judgment**.	9370

Wisdom

2:10-11	For **wisdom** will enter your heart, and knowledge will be pleasant to your soul. [11] Discretion will protect you, and understanding will guard you.	2683
3:13	Blessed is the man who finds **wisdom**, the man who gains understanding,	2683
10:23	A fool finds pleasure in evil conduct, but a man of understanding delights in **wisdom**.	2683
10:31	The mouth of the righteous brings forth **wisdom**, but a perverse tongue will be cut out.	2683
12:8	A man is praised according to his **wisdom**, but men with warped minds are despised.	8507
14:33	**Wisdom** reposes in the heart of the discerning and even among fools she lets herself be known.	2683
17:24	A discerning man keeps **wisdom** in view, but a fool's eyes wander to the ends of the earth.	2683
19:8	He who gets **wisdom** loves his own soul; he who cherishes understanding prospers.	4213
28:26	He who trusts in himself is a fool, but he who walks in **wisdom** is kept safe.	2683

Wise

1:5-6	let the **wise** listen and add to their learning, and let the discerning get guidance—[6] for understanding proverbs and parables, the sayings and riddles of the **wise**.	2682/2682
9:8-12	Do not rebuke a mocker or he will hate you; rebuke a **wise** man and he will love you. [9] Instruct a **wise** man and he will be wiser still; teach a righteous man and he will add to his learning. [10] "The fear of the LORD is the beginning of wisdom, and knowledge of the Holy One is understanding. [11] For through me your days will be many, and years will be added to your life. [12] If you are **wise**, your wisdom will reward you; if you are a mocker, you alone will suffer."	2682/2682/ 2681
10:8	The **wise** in heart accept commands, but a chattering fool comes to ruin.	2682
10:14	**Wise** men store up knowledge, but the mouth of a fool invites ruin.	2682
12:15	The way of a fool seems right to him, but a **wise** man listens to advice.	2682
13:20	He who walks with the **wise** grows **wise**, but a companion of fools suffers harm.	2682/2681
14:24	The wealth of the **wise** is their crown, but the folly of fools yields folly.	2682
15:24	The path of life leads upward for the **wise** to keep him from going down to the grave.	8505
21:22	A **wise** man attacks the city of the mighty and pulls down the stronghold in which they trust.	2682
24:5	A **wise** man has great power, and a man of knowledge increases strength;	2682
24:23	These also are sayings of the **wise**: To show partiality in judging is not good:	2682

WISDOM AND HUMILITY

Wisdom

11:2	When pride comes, then comes disgrace, but with humility comes **wisdom**.	2683
13:10	Pride only breeds quarrels, but **wisdom** is found in those who take advice.	2683

WISDOM AND THE FAMILY

Discerning

28:7	He who keeps the law is a **discerning** son, but a companion of gluttons disgraces his father.	1067

Judgment

3:21-22	My son, preserve sound **judgment** and discernment, do not let them out of your sight; [22] they will be life for you, an ornament to grace your neck.	9370

Knowledge

5:1-2	My son, pay attention to my wisdom, listen well to my words of insight, [2] that you may maintain discretion and your lips may preserve **knowledge**.	1981
19:27	Stop listening to instruction, my son, and you will stray from the words of **knowledge**.	1981

Understanding

4:1-2   Listen, my sons, to a father's instruction; pay attention and   1069
         gain **understanding**. [2] I give you sound learning, so do not
         forsake my teaching.

Wisdom

29:3   A man who loves **wisdom** brings joy to his father, but a com-   2683
         panion of prostitutes squanders his wealth.

Wise

10:1   The proverbs of Solomon: A **wise** son brings joy to his father,
         but a foolish son grief to his mother.   2682

10:5   He who gathers crops in summer is a **wise** son, but he who   8505
         sleeps during harvest is a disgraceful son.

13:1   A **wise** son heeds his father's instruction, but a mocker does not 2682
         listen to rebuke.

14:1   The **wise** woman builds her house, but with her own hands the   2682
         foolish one tears hers down.

15:20   A **wise** son brings joy to his father, but a foolish man despises 2682
         his mother.

17:2   A **wise** servant will rule over a disgraceful son, and will share 8505
         the inheritance as one of the brothers.

23:15   My son, if your heart is **wise**, then my heart will be glad;   2681

23:19   Listen, my son, and be **wise**, and keep your heart on the right   2681
         path.

23:24   The father of a righteous man has great joy; he who has a **wise** 2682
         son delights in him.

27:11   Be **wise**, my son, and bring joy to my heart; then I can answer   2681
         anyone who treats me with contempt.

CONTRASTS TO WISDOM

Again Proverbs uses contrasts to sharpen our acuteness in discerning between skillful and inept living. A key diagnostic test revealing the character of our hearts is whether or not we note and apply the contrasts between foolishness and wickedness. Wise individuals learn through their ears, whereas the fool learns only through the pain that moral stupidity brings. "For although they knew God, they neither glorified him as God nor gave thanks to him, but their thinking became futile and their foolish hearts were darkened" (Rom. 1:21).

WISDOM CONTRASTED TO THE WICKED		REFERENCE NUMBERS
Evil		
28:5	**Evil** men do not understand justice, but those who seek the LORD understand it fully.	8273
Strays		
21:16	A man who **strays** from the path of understanding comes to rest in the company of the dead.	9494
Unfaithful		
13:15	Good understanding wins favor, but the way of the **unfaithful** is hard.	953
22:12	The eyes of the LORD keep watch over knowledge, but he frustrates the words of the **unfaithful**.	953
Warped		
12:8	A man is praised according to his wisdom, but men with **warped** minds are despised.	6390
Wicked		
4:19	But the way of the **wicked** is like deep darkness; they do not know what makes them stumble.	8401
21:12	The Righteous One takes note of the house of the **wicked** and brings the **wicked** to ruin.	8401/8401
29:7	The righteous care about justice for the poor, but the **wicked** have no such concern.	8401

WISDOM CONTRASTED TO THE SINS OF THE TONGUE		
Folly		
14:29	A patient man has great understanding, but a quick-tempered man displays **folly**.	222
Fool		
10:8	The wise in heart accept commands, but a chattering **fool** comes to ruin.	211
10:14	Wise men store up knowledge, but the mouth of a **fool** invites ruin.	211
10:21	The lips of the righteous nourish many, but **fools** die for lack of judgment.	211
12:23	A prudent man keeps his knowledge to himself, but the heart of **fools** blurts out folly.	4067
15:2	The tongue of the wise commends knowledge, but the mouth of the **fool** gushes folly.	4067
15:7	The lips of the wise spread knowledge; not so the hearts of **fools**.	4067

15:14	The discerning heart seeks knowledge, but the mouth of a **fool** feeds on folly.	4067
17:28	Even a **fool** is thought wise if he keeps silent, and discerning if he holds his tongue.	211
23:9	Do not speak to a **fool**, for he will scorn the wisdom of your words.	4067
24:7	Wisdom is too high for a **fool**; in the assembly at the gate he has nothing to say.	211

Foolish

14:7	Stay away from a **foolish** man, for you will not find knowledge on his lips.	4067

Heart

15:7	The lips of the wise spread knowledge; not so the **hearts** of fools.	4213

Judgment

11:12	A man who lacks **judgment** derides his neighbor, but a man of understanding holds his tongue.	4213

Mouth

10:32	The lips of the righteous know what is fitting, but the **mouth** of the wicked only what is perverse.	7023
11:9	With his **mouth** the godless destroys his neighbor, but through knowledge the righteous escape.	7023
15:2	The tongue of the wise commends knowledge, but the **mouth** of the fool gushes folly.	7023
15:14	The discerning heart seeks knowledge, but the **mouth** of a fool feeds on folly.	7023

Talk

14:3	A fool's **talk** brings a rod to his back, but the lips of the wise protect them.	7023

Tongue

10:31	The mouth of the righteous brings forth wisdom, but a perverse **tongue** will be cut out.	4383

Words

10:19	When **words** are many, sin is not absent, but he who holds his tongue is wise.	1821
12:18	Reckless **words** pierce like a sword, but the tongue of the wise brings healing.	1051

WISDOM CONTRASTED TO THE FOOL

Folly

15:21	**Folly** delights a man who lacks judgment, but a man of understanding keeps a straight course.	222

Fool

1:22	"How long will you simple ones love your simple ways? How long will mockers delight in mockery and **fools** hate knowledge?"	4067
10:23	A **fool** finds pleasure in evil conduct, but a man of understanding delights in wisdom.	4067
11:29	He who brings trouble on his family will inherit only wind, and the **fool** will be servant to the wise.	211
12:15	The way of a **fool** seems right to him, but a wise man listens to advice.	211
13:16	Every prudent man acts out of knowledge, but a **fool** exposes his folly.	4067

REFERENCE
NUMBERS

13:20	He who walks with the wise grows wise, but a companion of **fools** suffers harm.	4067
14:8	The wisdom of the prudent is to give thought to their ways, but the folly of **fools** is deception.	4067
14:16	A wise man fears the LORD and shuns evil, but a **fool** is hot-headed and reckless.	4067
14:24	The wealth of the wise is their crown, but the folly of **fools** yields folly.	4067
14:33	Wisdom reposes in the heart of the discerning and even among **fools** she lets herself be known.	4067
17:16	Of what use is money in the hand of a **fool**, since he has no desire to get wisdom?	4067
17:24	A discerning man keeps wisdom in view, but a **fool's** eyes wander to the ends of the earth.	4067
18:2	A **fool** finds no pleasure in understanding but delights in airing his own opinions.	4067
26:12	Do you see a man wise in his own eyes? There is more hope for a **fool** than for him.	4067
28:26	He who trusts in himself is a **fool**, but he who walks in wisdom is kept safe.	4067
29:11	A **fool** gives full vent to his anger, but a wise man keeps himself under control.	4067

Foolish

10:1	The proverbs of Solomon: A wise son brings joy to his father, but a **foolish** son grief to his mother.	4067
14:1	The wise woman builds her house, but with her own hands the **foolish** one tears hers down.	222
15:20	A wise son brings joy to his father, but a **foolish** man despises his mother.	4067

Mocker

9:12	"If you are wise, your wisdom will reward you; if you are a **mocker**, you alone will suffer."	4329
14:6	The **mocker** seeks wisdom and finds none, but knowledge comes easily to the discerning.	4370
29:8	**Mockers** stir up a city, but wise men turn away anger.	408 + 4371

Simple

14:18	The **simple** inherit folly, but the prudent are crowned with knowledge.	7343

WISDOM CONTRASTED TO HATRED OF DISCIPLINE

Correction

12:1	Whoever loves discipline loves knowledge, but he who hates **correction** is stupid.	9350
15:12	A mocker resents **correction**; he will not consult the wise.	3519

Discipline

1:7	The fear of the LORD is the beginning of knowledge, but fools despise wisdom and **discipline**.	4592
15:32	He who ignores **discipline** despises himself, but whoever heeds correction gains understanding.	4592

Disgraces

29:15	The rod of correction imparts wisdom, but a child left to himself **disgraces** his mother.	1017

Lashes
17:10   A rebuke impresses a man of discernment more than a hundred   5782
lashes a fool.

Mocker
9:8   Do not rebuke a **mocker** or he will hate you; rebuke a wise man   4370
and he will love you.

13:1   A wise son heeds his father's instruction, but a **mocker** does   4370
not listen to rebuke.

Punished
21:11   When a mocker is **punished**, the simple gain wisdom; when a   6740
wise man is instructed, he gets knowledge.

Punishment
16:22   Understanding is a fountain of life to those who have it, but fol-   4592
ly brings **punishment** to fools.

Rod
10:13   Wisdom is found on the lips of the discerning, but a **rod** is for   8657
the back of him who lacks judgment.

26:3   A whip for the horse, a halter for the donkey, and a **rod** for the   8657
backs of fools!

INDEX

Moody Press, a ministry of the Moody Bible Institute,
is designed for education, evangelization, and edification.
If we may assist you in knowing more about Christ
and the Christian life, please write us without obligation:
Moody Press, c/o MLM, Chicago, Illinois 60610.